Creative DRINKS WITHOUT ALCOHOL

Arthur Weidmann

EXLEY

*Chocolate Ginger – Chocolate "Anna" – Drinking Chocolate
(in cup) – Chocolat a l'Orange – Chocolate Tornado*

Contents

Thanks

— to my colleagues on this book, the Weidmann's Creative and Media Cookery team, Bellevue au Lac, Sursee:
Rolf Brunner, chef
Ruth Kueng, stylist and food photographer
Margrith Streit, recipe creator
Claudia Wuest, journalist
for their creative, competent, and unflagging commitment to the success of this pleasurable work.

It was a pleasure to compose, vary, taste, change, and make the most of the ingredients both of Nature's rich garden and also to find new and tasty uses for the excellent products on the drinks market.
I hope that you will make frequent use of this book — both for your personal pleasure in realizing delicious ideas and so that you reap well-earned compliments.

A.W.

First published in Great Britain in 1989 by
Exley Publications Ltd
16 Chalk Hill, Watford, Herts WD1 4BN, United Kingdom.

Translation copyright © Exley Publications Ltd, 1989
Illustrations copyright © Albert Müller Verlag, 1987

British Library Cataloguing in Publication Data
Weidmann, Arthur.
   Creative drinks without alcohol.
   1. Soft drinks. Recipes.
   I. Title.
   II. Kreative Drinks ohne Alcohol. *English.*
   641.8'75

ISBN 1-85015-163-6

Translation: Frank Monaghan.
Typeset by Brush Off Studios, St Albans, Herts AL3 4PH.
Printed and bound in Hungary.

Foreword

The predominance that alcoholic drinks have enjoyed until now is largely due to the relative scarcity of equally attractive, enjoyable and tasty alcohol-free alternatives. "Creative Drinks Without Alcohol" is an attempt to help bridge that gap; you will notice a positive difference both visually and in taste between the alcohol-free drinks presented here and their tipsy-making predecessors.

Alcohol-free drinks can be just as much or even more fun; they can perk you up and do you good at the same time, keep you on your feet without sending you to sleep later, keep you young and fit, they are conducive to keeping your skin and system both healthy and supple. Objectively speaking, hangover-free drinking is not a loss but an enormous gain accompanied by many wholesome and beneficial side effects.

The book fits in with our changing lifestyles: with its health-oriented philosophy and its many recipes tailored to the needs of those thinking of their waistlines. For the "fire waters" alone that dominate the average cocktail mean an extra 100 to 250 calories for the consumer every time!

With this book and its bright, cheery and aromatic drinks we can toast "your good health" with a clear conscience and in the truest meaning of the words.

Arthur Weidmann

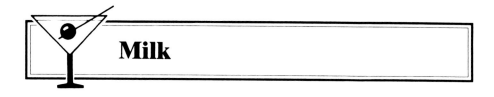

Milk

Milk in delicious variations

Milk is one of the oldest drinks and has always been one of our most important foodstuffs. It continues to play a dominant role in today's diet too. Milk contains a healthy balance of all the essential nutrients that the body needs. One pint of milk can provide us with a quarter of our daily requirements of proteins and fat and half of the essential minerals of phosphorous and calcium. Milk also contains 15 of the 20 known vitamins that supply our systems with essential antibodies.

Milk can be used to make particularly aromatic drinks. Because it can easily blend in with other scents and tastes, milk can assume practically any aroma. When creating milk drinks there are no limits to what the imagination can do. On hot days, you can mix a whole range of drinks which are just as delicious as the highly popular thirst-quenching milk shakes or frappés and which can act as both a change and a treat.

But hot or cold, all milk drinks have one thing in common: they provide energy for the body and supply it with essential nutrients.

Caramel Cream	*1½ tbsps sugar* *2 tbsps water* *150 ml (6 fl.oz) pasteurized milk* *50 ml (2 fl.oz) cream*	Heat the sugar until brown, add water and milk and bring to the boil. Leave to chill. Whip the cream and fold into the mixture.
Apricot Milk	*4 apricots* *150 ml (6 fl.oz) pasteurized milk*	Mix the ingredients together and serve immediately.
Banana Froth	*100 ml (4 fl.oz) pasteurized milk* *1 banana* *½ cup crushed ice* *sugar to taste*	Mix the ingredients until thick and frothy. Serve in tall glasses.
Grenadine Dream	*200 ml (8 fl.oz) pasteurized milk* *3 tbsps grenadine syrup*	Mix.
Cucumber Milk	*⅛ of a cucumber* *a pinch of dill* *¼ of an onion* *juice of ½ a lemon* *salt, sugar, pepper* *150 ml (6 fl.oz) pasteurized milk*	Peel the cucumber and onion. Blend with the dill, lemon juice and milk. Season. Garnish with a little dill and serve chilled.
Roast Nut Milkshake	*2 tbsps finely grated* * candied hazelnuts* *200 ml (8 fl.oz) pasteurized milk* *50 ml (2 fl.oz) cream* *ice cubes*	Mix the hazelnuts with the milk and cream and serve with ice.
Blackcurrant Milkshake	*200 ml (8 fl.oz) pasteurized milk* *2 tbsps blackcurrant jam* *sugar to taste* *3 tbsps cream*	Mix the ingredients together. Chill and serve.
Beauty Cup	*150 ml (6 fl.oz) pasteurized milk* *½ tbsp rose-hip jam* *juice of ½ a lemon*	Whip the ingredients together. Pour into a glass and serve immediately.

parsley, chives, herbs 1 tbsp steamed spinach salt, ground spice 200 ml (8 fl.oz) pasteurized milk	Mix the ingredients and serve immediately. To chill add 2 ice cubes.	**Spring Cocktail**
250 ml (9 fl.oz) pasteurized milk ¼ tsp crushed aniseed 2 tbsps sugar ½ tsp cornflour (cornstarch)	Heat the milk, aniseed and sugar and leave to stand for 5 minutes. Mix the cornflour (cornstarch) with a little water and add. Stir, leave to stand for a further 5 minutes. Strain and serve.	**Aniseed Milk**
200 ml (8 fl.oz) pasteurized milk 1 tsp sugar ¼ tsp powdered sage	Heat the milk, add the sugar and sage. Stir and serve. Delicious cold, too.	**Sage Milk**
200 ml (8 fl.oz) pasteurized milk 2 tbsps blackcurrant syrup ice cubes	Whip the milk and blackcurrant syrup together. Serve with ice.	**Blackcurrant Milk**
1 tbsp lemon juice 2 tbsps orange juice a little grated lemon rind 200 ml (8 fl.oz) pasteurized milk	Blend the lemon and orange juice with the lemon rind and sugar. Add to the milk, beating well.	**Caesar**
1 egg 1 banana 1 tbsp honey 200 ml (8 fl.oz) pasteurized milk	Mix all the ingredients together.	**Liquid Energy**
150 ml (6 fl.oz) tomato juice 150 ml (6 fl.oz) pasteurized milk pepper, salt, ground spices	Mix the tomato juice and milk. Season with pepper, salt and ground spices.	**Adam**
200 ml (8 fl.oz) pasteurized milk 30 g (1 oz) marzipan sugar to taste	Mix.	**Mandorle**

Magic Milk

1 egg
2 tbsps honey
3 tbsps Ovaltine
200 ml (8 fl.oz) pasteurized milk

Gradually add milk to the other ingredients and blend together.

Happy Easter

1 tbsp cress and parsley
1 tbsp cream cheese
4 drops lemon juice
salt, pepper
200 ml (8 fl.oz) pasteurized milk

Finely chop the cress and parsley. Mix with the cream cheese and lemon juice. Season with salt and pepper. Top up with milk.

Elisabetha

3 tbsps apricot purée
a little lemon juice
1 tbsp honey
200 ml (8 fl.oz) pasteurized milk

Mix all the ingredients together well.

Strawberry Fruit Milk

50 g (2 oz) strawberries
150 ml (6 fl.oz) pasteurized milk
1-2 tbsps sugar
½ tbsp lemon juice

Wash and prepare the strawberries. Mix together with the milk, sugar and lemon juice. Chill well and serve.

Apple Drink

½ an apple
honey to taste
150 ml (6 fl.oz) pasteurized milk

Grate the apple. Mix with the honey and milk.

Maple Cup

150 ml (6 fl.oz) pasteurized milk
1½ tbsps maple syrup
juice of ½ a lemon

Whip the milk and maple syrup. Add the lemon juice until the milk thickens slightly.

Egg Flip

½ an egg
125 ml (5 fl.oz) pasteurized milk
1 tbsp brown sugar
nutmeg

Beat the egg until frothy. Heat the milk, add the egg, stirring well. Heat in a double boiler, add sugar, stir. Pour into glasses and sprinkle with nutmeg.

Berry Milkshake

150 g (5 oz) raspberry and
   redcurrant yogurt
300 ml (10 fl.oz) milk
redcurrants to decorate

Whip together the yogurt and milk until frothy. Pour into tall glasses and decorate with redcurrants.

 Caramel Cream – Apricot Milk – Banana Froth –
Grenadine Dream – Savoury Cucumber Milk

Busy Bee

200 ml (8 fl.oz) pasteurized milk
1 tbsp honey
a few drops of lemon juice
ice cubes

Beat the milk, honey, and lemon juice together well. Serve with ice cubes.

Lemon Milk

3 tsps sugar
grated lemon rind
2 tbsps lemon juice
200 ml (8 fl.oz) pasteurized milk

Slowly add the sugar, lemon rind and lemon juice to the milk. Beat well. Serve immediately.

Apple and Cinnamon Milk

½ an apple
some lemon juice
1-2 tbsps sugar
150 ml (6 fl.oz) pasteurized milk
¼ tsp cinnamon
a slice of orange

Peel and core the apple. Cut into slices. Purée with the lemon juice, sugar and milk. Add the cinnamon and chill. Garnish with a slice of orange and serve immediately.

Café Noisette

1 tsp coffee
2 tbsps boiling water
sugar to taste
1 tbsp chopped hazelnuts
150 ml (6 fl.oz) milk
1 tbsp cream

Dissolve the coffee in the boiling water and blend together with the rest of the ingredients except the cream. Pour into a glass and decorate with cream.

Minted Orange Cups

4 slices of orange, unpeeled
150 ml (6 fl.oz) fresh orange juice
600 ml (20 fl.oz) chilled milk
2 tbsps whipped cream
fresh mint leaves

Cut each orange slice from the middle to the outside edge and slot over the rims of four glasses. Whip the orange juice and milk together well. Pour into glasses and top with whipped cream and mint leaves.

Yogurt Strawberry Cooler

150 g (5 oz) strawberry yogurt
300 ml (10 fl.oz) chilled milk
crushed strawberries

Whip the yogurt and milk together well. Pour into two glasses and decorate with crushed strawberries.

Ice Cream

Ice Cream drinks are soft and full of surprises

The history of ice cream stretches further back into the past than we would ever dream. People have eaten ice cream for much longer than we have had refrigerators in our kitchens. The Chinese have known how to sweeten up their lives with it for over 3000 years. Hippocrates the Greek voiced his opinion that ice had healing properties some 300 years before Christ. He used to prescribe ice cream, as it were, as medicine against various ills. The Roman Emperor Nero, the Venetian trader Marco Polo and many other famous historical figures have all feasted on a cool and creamy ice cream.

Ice cream can be used and enjoyed in a multitude of ways. Many drinks can be enriched and given a refreshing twist with this delicacy made from milk, cream and eggs. Ice cream can be mixed with practically anything, not just with milk. Combine it with fruit juices, syrups, sparkling mineral waters or coffee to produce refreshing and invigorating drinks. Special effects can be achieved by mixing ice cream with warm drinks.

So, you can create cocktails packed full of delicious surprises.

Cold Currant
40 g (1½ oz) redcurrant syrup
1 scoop vanilla ice cream
100 ml (4 fl.oz) milk
2 tbsps cream

Mix all the ingredients together. Pour into a glass, stir and serve.

Orange Cooler
2 scoops vanilla ice cream
1 tbsp orange syrup
100 ml (4 fl.oz) milk

Put the ice cream and orange syrup into a glass. Fill with milk. Stir and serve with a straw.

Banana Fresh
1 scoop vanilla ice cream
½ a ripe banana
the juice and rind of a lemon
2 tsps sugar
150 ml (6 fl.oz) milk

Mix all the ingredients together.

Vienna Glow
2 small scoops vanilla ice cream
100 ml (4 fl.oz) hot coffee
nutmeg
1 tbsp whipping cream
1 tsp chocolate vermicelli

Put 1 scoop of ice cream into a glass, pour on half the coffee and sprinkle with nutmeg. Add second scoop of ice cream and remaining coffee. Top with whipped cream and vermicelli.

Maple Fizz
2 tbsps maple syrup
4 tbsps cream
3 crushed ice cubes
1 scoop nut ice cream
50 ml (2 fl.oz) mineral water

Shake the syrup, cream, and ice together and pour into a glass. Add ice cream and fill glass with mineral water.

Melon Shake
¼ of a honeydew melon
3 tbsps milk
1 tsp lemon juice
1 tsp sugar
2 scoops vanilla ice cream

Pare and seed the melon, cut into pieces. Mix all the ingredients together. Pour into a glass and serve.

Apple Cream
1 scoop vanilla ice cream
150 ml (6 fl.oz) apple juice
grated nutmeg

Mix the ice cream and apple juice together. Pour into a glass and sprinkle with nutmeg.

Cold Currant – Orange Cooler – Banana Fresh

Ginger Haze
150 ml (6 fl.oz) ginger ale
1 scoop lemon ice cream
fresh mint
maraschino cherry

Pour the ginger ale into a glass. Top with lemon ice cream. Garnish with mint and cherry.

Crème de Fraises
5 strawberries
1 scoop strawberry ice cream
100 ml (4 fl.oz) milk
sugar to taste
a few drops of lemon juice

Wash and prepare the strawberries. Mix with the ice cream, sugar, lemon juice and milk. Serve immediately.

Orange Frost
150 ml (6 fl.oz) orange juice
1 scoop orange or mandarin
   ice cream

Mix until frothy. Serve in a glass.

Almond Shake
150 ml (6 fl.oz) milk
1 scoop vanilla ice cream
25 g (1 oz) marzipan
2-3 drops almond essence

Mix all the ingredients together. Pour into a glass and serve.

Chocolate Shake
100 ml (4 fl.oz) milk
2 scoops chocolate ice cream
1 tbsp chocolate powder

Mix all the ingredients together. Pour into a glass and serve.

Tomato Shake
70 ml (3 fl.oz) milk
70 ml (3 fl.oz) tomato juice
2 small scoops lemon ice cream
Salt, pepper

Mix all the ingredients together. Pour into a glass and serve.

Ginger Ice
100 ml (4 fl.oz) ginger ale
1 scoop vanilla ice cream
½ a slice of pineapple
1 tbsp pineapple juice
a pinch of ground ginger

Mix all the ingredients together. Pour into a glass and serve.

Hot Rhythm
100 ml (4 fl.oz) milk
1 scoop vanilla ice cream
1 scoop chocolate ice cream
1 tsp instant coffee
½ of a banana

Mix all the ingredients together. Pour into a glass and serve immediately.

 Ginger Haze – Creme de Fraises – Orange Frost

Bilberry	*1 bilberry yogurt* *1 tsp sugar* *1 scoop vanilla ice cream* *100 ml (4 fl.oz) milk*	Stir all the ingredients together. Serve immediately.
Mocha Frappé	*1 scoop coffee ice cream* *1 heaped tsp instant coffee* *1 scoop vanilla ice cream* *100 ml (4 fl.oz) milk*	Mix all the ingredients together.
Pineapple Cream Shake	*100 ml (4 fl.oz) pineapple juice* *1 scoop lemon sorbet* *50 ml (2 fl.oz) cream*	Mix all the ingredients together and serve chilled.
Mocha Ice Cream	*150 ml (6 fl.oz) expresso coffee* *1 tbsp sugar* *1 drop angostura bitters* *1 scoop coffee ice cream* *1 tbsp cream*	Sweeten the coffee and season with angostura. Put the ice cream into a glass. Pour in the coffee and top with cream.
Marilyn	*1 peach* *1 scoop vanilla ice cream* *2 tbsps lemon juice* *1 tbsp cream* *100 ml (4 fl.oz) milk*	Pare and purée the peach. Mix together with ice cream and lemon juice. Add milk and cream and whip.
Blackberry Mix	*50 g (2 oz) blackberries* *1 tbsp sugar* *1 tbsp cream* *100 ml (4 fl.oz) milk* *2 scoops blackberry or* * strawberry ice cream*	Mix all the ingredients together.

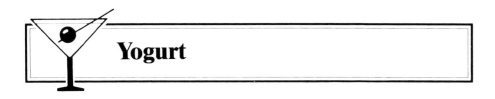

Yogurt

50 Types of Yogurt to Mix

Yogurt has been available in Central Europe since the beginning of this century. Originally, this dairy product came from Asia Minor and the Balkans, where it was made from sheep's, goat's or buffalo's milk. Yogurt (and cheese) were, for a long time, the only preservable milk products known in these regions and so were of great importance.

Yogurt only became a popular health food with the introduction of fruit yogurts in the fifties and it has come to play an important role in modern nutrition. Today, this protein-rich product with its slightly sour taste is available set, stirred or in liquid form. Constantly changing and often surprising variations of tastes and combinations of different fruits are appearing on the market. Alongside natural yogurts and the ever-popular strawberry and raspberry varieties more exotic ingredients such as kiwi fruit, coconut and mango have been accepted. However, it is not only the different varieties that are designed to meet individual tastes. Yogurt is now available with different fat content levels in full cream, skimmed or semi-skimmed varieties and artificially sweetened in the form of low-calorie diet yogurt.

Even more numerous than the different varieties and tastes are the ways of using yogurt. It does not always occur to people that apart from in desserts, this dairy product can also be used to make delicious and light summer drinks. The many types of yogurt make it possible to have an enormous variety of refreshing drinks.

"Southern" Yogurt	*90 g (4 oz) natural yogurt* *juice of an orange* *juice of ½ a grapefruit* *1 tbsp banana purée*	Beat the ingredients together well.
Early Starter	*90g (4 oz) natural yogurt* *100 ml (4 fl.oz) beetroot juice* *chives* *garlic powder* *celery salt*	Mix the yogurt and beetroot juice. Chop the parsley and chives very finely and stir in. Season with garlic powder and celery salt to taste.
Citronelle	*The flesh of 1 lemon* *1 scoop of lemon sorbet* *100 ml (4 fl.oz) lemon* *drinking yogurt* *1 ice cube*	Quickly mix all the ingredients together and serve immediately.
Reddy Mix	*100 g (4 oz) natural yogurt* *50 ml (2 fl.oz) milk* *50 g (2 oz) redcurrants* *1 tsp raspberry purée* *1½ tbsps of sugar* *ice cubes*	Mix the ingredients together. Strain and serve immediately.
Carrot Yogurt	*100 g (4 oz) natural yogurt* *1 tbsp sugar* *100 ml (4 fl.oz) carrot juice*	Beat the ingredients together well and serve.
Tomato Yogurt	*100 ml (4 fl.oz) natural yogurt* *50 ml (2 fl.oz) milk* *1 tbsp tomato purée* *a pinch of salt and pepper* *ice cubes*	Beat the ingredients together. Serve with ice.
Honey Yogurt	*150 ml (6 fl.oz) natural yogurt* *50 ml (2 fl.oz) milk* *1½ tbsp liquid honey*	Shake the ingredients well and serve immediately.

"Southern" Yogurt – Early Starter – Citronelle

Sour Apple	100 g (4 oz) natural yogurt 100 ml (4 fl.oz) apple juice 1 tbsp cream 1½ tbsp sugar juice of ½ a lemon 1 ice cube	Mix all the ingredients together.
Mocha Pear	½ a pear 100 ml (4 fl.oz) coffee drinking yogurt 50 ml (2 fl.oz) milk sugar to taste 1 tbsp drinking chocolate powder 1 ice cube	Mix all the ingredients together and serve immediately.
Apricotine	100 ml (4 fl.oz) apricot drinking yogurt 50 ml (2 fl.oz) condensed milk sugar to taste	Shake the ingredients and serve immediately.
Yogurt-Soda	90 g (4 fl.oz) raspberry yogurt 2 tbsps raspberry syrup 100 ml (4 fl.oz) mineral water	Mix all the ingredients together and serve cold.
Apple Cup	150 ml (6 fl.oz) lemon drinking yogurt ½ an apple a pinch of cinnamon sugar to taste	Peel and grate the apple. Mix with the drinking yogurt and cinnamon. Sweeten to taste.
Apricot Sparkle	100 ml (4 fl.oz) apricot drinking yogurt 50 ml (2 fl.oz) apple juice 50 ml (2 fl.oz) mineral water 3 ice cubes	Pour the yogurt into a glass and top up with apple juice and mineral water.
Melta	100 ml (4 fl.oz) peach juice 1 tbsp lemon juice 100 ml (4 fl.oz) raspberry drinking yogurt 1 ice cube	Shake the ingredients and serve immediately.

150 ml (6 fl.oz) coffee drinking yogurt 50 ml (2 fl.oz) cold coffee sugar to taste 1 tbsp cream chocolate vermicelli	Shake the yogurt and coffee together well and sweeten to taste. Whip the cream until stiff and use to top the drink. Sprinkle with chocolate.	**Expresso**
150 ml (6 fl.oz) strawberry drinking yogurt 50 ml (2 fl.oz) cold coffee cinnamon, pepper, ground cloves 2 strawberries	Stir the yogurt and spices together. Wash, prepare and cut the stawberries into four and put into a glass. Fill up with yogurt and serve with a spoon.	**Strawberry Spice**
1 scoop of vanilla ice cream 100 ml (4 fl.oz) raspberry drinking yogurt 1 tbsp raspberry syrup ice cubes	Mix the ingredients together and serve immediately.	**Raspberry Dream**
90 g (4 oz) bilberry yogurt 100 ml (4 fl.oz) milk 50 g (2 oz) blackberries 1 tbsp sugar to taste	Stir the milk and yogurt together. Put the blackberries into a glass, sweeten and pour on the liquid. Serve with a spoon.	**Blackberry**
2 tbsps ground almonds 100 ml (4 fl.oz) natural yogurt 50 ml (2 fl.oz) cream 1 tsp each honey and sugar a few drops of lemon juice 1 ice cube ½ tsp chocolate vermicelli	Mix all the ingredients together, except the vermicelli. Pour into a glass and sprinkle with the chocolate vermicelli.	**Yogurt "Nocciole"**
150 ml (6 fl.oz) lemon drinking yogurt 1 orange 1 ice cube sugar to taste	Cut the orange in half. Cut off one slice and squeeze the remaining fruit. Mix the orange juice and yogurt together. Sweeten to taste and add the ice. Decorate glass with the slice of orange and serve.	**Yogurt a l'Orange**

Pear Cup

½ a pear
150 ml (6 fl. oz) natural yogurt
3 tbsps milk
1 tbsp thick pear juice

Peel and core the pear. Mix with the other ingredients and serve.

Banana Fun

100 ml (6 fl. oz) natural yogurt
50 ml (2 fl. oz) milk
½ a ripe banana
1 tbsp sugar
1 ice cube

Mix all the ingredients together and serve immediately.

Good Morning

100 ml (4 fl. oz) redcurrant juice
1 tsp ground nuts
100 ml (4 fl. oz) natural yogurt
1 tbsp sugar
ice cubes

Mix the ingredients together and serve chilled.

Pussycat

100 ml (4 fl. oz) natural yogurt
50 ml (2 fl. oz) milk
a pinch of ginger
1 tbsp cranberry jam
1 ice cube

Shake the yogurt, milk, ginger and cranberry jam together. Put the ice into a glass, pour in the mixture and serve.

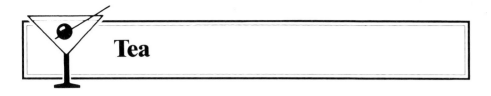

Tea

Tea, a stimulating or relaxing pleasure

Long before international travel was common, tea had already grown popular in every corner of the world. The best proof of this is that, today, tea is drunk more often than any other drink, whether for pleasure or for medicinal reasons! Tea-drinking began almost five thousand years ago in China. The sea-faring nations took the "excellent herb" to Europe at the start of the 17th century. For a long time the market was dominated almost exclusively by China tea. It was only at the turn of the century that the Englishman, Sir Thomas Lipton, introduced Ceylon tea. After a visit to Sri Lanka, the English pioneer bought large pieces of land in Ceylon and planted tea which he then imported directly into Europe. This made it possible for him to put his Lipton tea on the market in England and soon after across the world at prices that even the working class could afford. What had once been the "diplomats' drink" became the "national drink". Today, most tea consumed in Europe and the U.S.A. comes from Ceylon.

However, it is not only the variety of places where it is grown that means that the choice of teas is now so enormous, but also the careful blending of the various types: there are more than 1500 varieties. It should not be forgotten that tea can be an excellent ingredient for many delicious drinks which can be enjoyed both hot and cold.

In spite of the many differences in taste, however, all teas have one thing in common; they are stimulating without being irritating – but they can also have a calming effect depending on how they are prepared. For the tea to be stimulating it should only draw for two to three minutes. If the tea is to be relaxing, then it must draw for more than three minutes as the tannic acid is not released until after the caffeine and reduces its effects; however, it is at this point that the tea begins to taste slightly bitter. Caffeine works directly on the brain and central nervous system; increased powers of concentration after drinking tea can be traced back to this.

Camolem   70 ml (3 fl.oz) cold camomile tea
2 scoops lemon sorbet
50 ml (2 fl.oz) apple juice

Shake the ingredients well.

Mincitrus   100 ml (4 fl.oz) cold peppermint
    tea
50 ml (2 fl.oz) orange juice
2 tbsps grapefruit juice
1 tbsp lemon juice
sugar to taste
2-3 drops angostura bitters

Mix the tea and the other ingredients together well.

Legrape   150 ml (6 fl.oz) cold lime balm tea
30 g (1 oz) grapefruit syrup
1 tbsp lemon juice

Stir the ingredients well together.

Fruca   70 ml (3 fl.oz) fruit peel tea
70 ml (3 fl.oz) lemon drinking
    yogurt
50 ml (2 fl.oz) carrot juice
1 tbsp honey

Stir all the ingredients together well.

Camocassi   1 camomile tea bag
100 ml (4 fl.oz) water
100 ml (4 fl.oz) blackcurrant juice
¼ tsp ginger
sugar to taste

Bring the water and blackcurrant juice to the boil. Pour on to the tea bag and let it stand for a while. Sweeten to taste.

Lemon Balm   100 ml (4 fl.oz) lemon balm tea
1 egg
½ tsp vanilla sugar
50 ml (2 fl.oz) milk

Mix all the ingredients together.

Mango Spice Bath   1½ tsp tropical mango tea
175 ml (7 fl.oz) boiling water
1 pinch each cardamom, aniseed,
    ground cloves and cinnamon
sugar to taste
milk

Brew the tea and spices and leave to draw for 4 minutes. Strain, sweeten and serve with milk, if desired.

150 ml (6 fl.oz) lime blossom tea *40 g (1½ oz) redcurrant syrup* *1 tsp lemon juice*	Mix the lime blossom tea, syrup and lemon juice together.	**Limcurmon**
100 ml (4 fl.oz) strong, cold lime blossom tea *1 scoop vanilla ice cream* *1 scoop lemon sorbet* *50 ml (2 fl.oz) milk*	Mix the ingredients together and serve immediately.	**Limvamon**
150 ml (6 fl.oz) black tea *ground cloves, nutmeg, cinnamon* *1 tbsp honey* *50 ml (2 fl.oz) orange juice*	Brew the tea and spices and leave to draw for a while. Mix with remaining ingredients.	**Spiced Tea**
120 ml (5 fl.oz) cold black tea *1 slice pineapple* *1 scoop lemon sorbet* *sugar to taste*	Mix all the ingredients together.	**Pinemon Tea**
150 ml (6 fl.oz) cold rose hip tea *50 ml (2 fl.oz) grapefruit juice* *1 tsp lemon juice* *1 tsp thick pear juice*	Shake all the ingredients together well.	**Rograpear Tea**
250 ml (9 fl.oz) Twinings Apple Tea *250 ml (9 fl.oz) sparkling lemonade* *2 tbsps lemon juice* *sugar to taste* *crushed ice* *apple slices to garnish*	Brew the tea and allow to cool. Add the sparkling lemonade, lemon juice and sugar to taste. Pour over crushed ice and garnish with apple slices.	**Apple Cooler**
1 tsp Twinings Mandarin Tea *150 ml (6 fl.oz) water* *1 green apple* *5 drops lemon juice* *sugar to taste*	Peel the apple. Boil the peel in the water, let it draw briefly. Re-boil, add the tea and let it stand for 3 minutes. Strain and serve.	**Mandarin Apple**

Eastern Promise

600 ml (20 fl.oz) cold Twinings
    Jasmine Tea
2 tbsps orange juice
227 g (8 oz) can of pineapple in
    natural juice
250 ml (8 fl.oz) bitter lemon
crushed ice
orange slices

Mix together the tea, orange juice, pineapple juice and bitter lemon. Pour into four glasses with crushed ice and decorate with the pineapple pieces and orange slices.

Orange Tea

250 ml (8 fl.oz) cold Twinings
    Jasmine Tea
250 ml (8 fl.oz) orange juice
125 ml (4 fl.oz) sparkling
    lemonade
orange slices

Mix together the tea, orange juice and sparkling lemonade. Pour into four glasses with crushed ice and decorate each glass with an orange slice.

Cherry Fizz

600 ml (20 fl.oz) Twinings
    Wild Cherry Tea
600 ml (20 fl.oz) sparkling
    apple juice
4 tbsps blackcurrant cordial
1 sliced apple
a few strawberries, raspberries
    and cherries
ice cubes

Mix together the tea, apple juice and blackcurrant cordial in a jug. Top up with the fruit and ice cubes.

Ginger Up

300 mlk (10 fl.oz) Twinings
    Darjeeling Tea
300 ml (10 fl.oz) apple juice
ground ginger to taste
brown sugar to taste

Mix together the tea and apple juice and heat but do not boil. Add ground ginger and sugar to taste.

Earl Grey and Red

1 tsp Earl Grey
125 ml (5 fl.oz) boiling water
50 ml (2 fl.oz) redcurrant juice
a slice of lemon
sugar to taste

Let the tea draw for 3-5 minutes in the water and strain. Gently warm the currant juice. Add to the tea, sweeten and serve with a slice of lemon.

Ladies' Choice

1 tsp Earl Grey
125 ml (5 fl.oz) boiling water
50 ml (2 fl.oz) cream
1 egg yolk
½ tbsp sugar

Let the tea draw for 3-5 minutes in the water and strain. Beat the cream, egg yolk and sugar until slightly frothy. Add the tea, stir carefully until creamy in a double boiler and serve immediately.

Camolem – Mincitrus – Legrape

Tropicus	1 tsp tropical mango tea 150 ml (6 fl.oz) boiling water ¼ tsp hibiscus blossom 5 drops lemon juice sugar to taste	Let all the ingredients draw for 3-5 minutes in the water. Strain and sweeten to taste.
Grenada Time	1 tsp Twinings Mandarin Tea 150 ml (6 fl.oz) boiling water 1 tbsp grenadine syrup 1 tbsp whipped cream cinnamon sugar	Put the tea into the boiling water and let it draw for 3-4 minutes. Strain. Add syrup, sweeten with a little cinnamon sugar and serve topped with cream.
Mandarin Rose	1 tsp Twinings Mandarin Tea ½ tsp rose blossom leaves 175 ml (7 fl.oz) boiling water 1 tsp vanilla sugar	Let the tea and rose leaves draw for 3-5 minutes. Strain and sweeten.
Citrus Tea	100 ml (4 fl.oz) fruit peel tea 3 tbsps lemon juice 2 tbsps each grapefruit and 　　orange juice sugar to taste	Mix all the ingredients together well.
Menthe au Chocolat	150 ml (6 fl.oz) peppermint tea 2 tbsps liquid chocolate 2 tbsps cream flaked chocolate	Mix the peppermint tea and the chocolate together. Whip the cream until stiff and use to top the drink. Sprinkle with flaked chocolate.
Rose Hip Cream Tea	150 ml (6 fl.oz) rose hip tea sugar to taste 2 tbsps cream a little candied lemon peel 1 tbsp grated hazelnuts	Sweeten the tea to taste. Whip the cream until stiff. Chop the candied lemon very finely, fold into the cream with the hazelnuts and use to top the drink.
Cherry Lemon Crush	300 ml (10 fl.oz) Twinings 　　Wild Cherry Tea 300 ml (10 fl.oz) water 50 g (2 oz) fine sugar 1 lemon lemon slices ice cubes	Chop up the lemon and place in a blender with the sugar, water and some ice cubes. Blend until the lemon is crushed. Strain into a jug and top up with cherry tea. Divide mixture between four glasses, decorate with lemon slices and serve with ice cubes.

1 l (40 fl.oz) ice tea *100 ml (4 fl.oz) lemon juice* *½ tsp ground ginger* *½ tsp cinnamon* *3 cloves* *a pinch of cardamom* *2 tbsps peppermint syrup* *ice cubes*	Heat the lemon juice, syrup and spices. Leave to draw for 5 minutes and strain. Add the ice tea, mix well and serve with ice cubes.	**Oriental Ice Tea**
1 l (40 fl.oz) ice tea *400 ml (16 fl.oz) grapefruit juice* *200 ml (8 fl.oz) orange juice* *200 ml (8 fl.oz) white grape juice* *2 grapefruits* *5 tbsps sugar* *mineral water* *ice cubes*	Peel and prepare the grapefruit. Mix with the sugar. Mix the tea, juices and sliced fruits together well. Add ice cubes and mix with mineral water.	**Jaffa Punch Ice Tea**
1 l (40 fl.oz) ice tea *a pinch each of nutmeg,* * cinnamon, pimento* *2 tsps sugar* *100 ml (4 fl.oz) orange juice* *50 ml (2 fl.oz) lemon juice* *350 ml (14 fl.oz) bilberry juice* *ice cubes* *mineral water*	Bring the juices and spices to the boil and let it draw briefly. Chill, add ice cubes and ice tea and mix with mineral water.	**Bilberry Tea**
1 l (40 fl.oz) ice tea *250 g (10 oz) frozen strawberries* * (lightly sweetened)* *4 scoops lemon sorbet* *4 peppermint leaves, chopped* *ice cubes*	Put all the ingredients into a container and leave to stand briefly. Stir well and serve. Other frozen berries can be used instead of strawberries.	**Ice Fraise**

 Tropicus – Grenada Time – Mandarin Rose

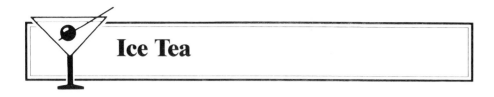

Ice Tea

The secret of making ice tea

Even in grandmother's day cold tea was drunk to quench the thirst on hot days. But cold tea bears absolutely no comparison to ice tea which has achieved real record turnovers in recent years. To prevent chilled tea from turning very dark and a thin oily film from forming on the surface use deep-freeze techniques. The shock of freezing preserves the full aroma and, above all, the tea's active agents completely. This drink can scarcely be compared to the average cold tea.

When making ice tea, the glasses should be two thirds filled with ice cubes and the fresh, still hot tea poured over it. As the tea is considerably weakened by the melted ice, it needs to be made at double strength. This is the way to make a refreshing, thirst-quenching and stimulating ice tea whose taste differs markedly from one left to chill or even stand. The taste of the ice tea can be varied by the choice of tea. But the addition of lemon juice or lemon slices allows you to produce subtle differences effortlessly. Many other drinks can be made using ice which make alcohol-free drinking both attractive and varied.

Lemsea   *850 ml (30 fl.oz) ice tea*
100 g (4 oz) lemon syrup
5 tbsps apple purée
ice cubes

Mix the ingredients well together and serve with ice.

Red Ice Tea   *600 ml (20 fl.oz) ice tea*
200 ml (8 fl.oz) redcurrant juice
200 ml (8 fl.oz) lemon mineral
  water
ice cubes

Mix the ice tea and redcurrant juice together. Top up with mineral water and serve with ice.

Iced Rasgrape   *700 ml (24 fl.oz) ice tea*
100 g (4 oz) raspberry syrup
200 ml (8 fl.oz) grapefruit juice
ice cubes

Stir the ingredients together and serve with ice.

Tomcel Tea   *600 ml (20 fl.oz) ice tea*
200 ml (8 fl.oz) tomato juice
200 ml (8 fl.oz) celery juice
a dash of Worcester sauce
ice cubes

Mix the ice tea and the juices together. Season with Worcester sauce and serve with ice.

Iceberry   *750 ml (26 fl.oz) ice tea*
100 g (4 oz) blackberries
100 g (4 oz) blackcurrant syrup
3 tbsps lemon juice
ice cubes

Mix all the ingredients together. Serve with ice.

Grape Ice Tea   *500 ml (17 fl.oz) ice tea*
400 ml (14 fl.oz) red grape juice
ground cloves, nutmeg
ice cubes

Mix the ingredients together. Serve with ice.

Peacamon Tea   *600 ml (20 fl.oz) ice tea*
400 ml (16 fl.oz) peach nectar
1 tsp cinnamon
ice cubes

Mix all the ingredients together well. Serve with ice.

Lemsea – Red Ice Tea – Iced Rasgrape – Tomcel Tea

Iced Strawberry Punch

800 ml (28 fl.oz) ice tea
200 g (8 oz) strawberries
pepper, cardamom
sugar to taste
2 tbsps lemon juice
ice cubes

Wash and prepare the strawberries. Mix with pepper, cardamom, sugar and lemon juice. Top up with ice tea and serve with ice.

Iced Lime Blossom

800 ml (28 fl.oz) ice tea
8 leaves each peppermint and
    lime balm
200 ml (8 fl.oz) cold lime blossom
    tea
ice cubes

Chop the peppermint and lime balm very finely. Stir into the lime blossom and ice tea. Serve with ice and a straw.

Iced Lemora

600 ml (20 fl.oz) ice tea
300 ml (10 fl.oz) orange juice
a little grated orange peel
100 ml (4 fl.oz) lemon juice
ice cubes

Mix all the ingredients well together. Serve with ice.

Ice Shake

600 ml (20 fl.oz) ice tea
4 scoops vanilla ice cream
50 ml (2 oz) cream
250 ml (9 fl.oz) apple juice
ice cubes

Shake all the ingredients well together and serve with ice.

Iced Limeapple

800 ml (28 fl.oz) ice tea
4 slices pineapple
100 ml (4 fl.oz) lime juice

Mix all the ingredients together. Serve with ice.

Pearcori

700 ml (24 fl.oz) ice tea
250 ml (9 fl.oz) pear nectar
50 ml (2 fl.oz) lemon juice
ice cubes

Shake the ingredients well. Serve with ice.

Aprimond

500 ml (17 fl.oz) ice tea
10 apricots
5 drops almond essence
200 ml (8 fl.oz) mineral water
ice cubes

Wash and halve the apricots. Mix with the iced tea, add the almond essence and top up with mineral water. Serve with ice.

Warm Coffee

Fresh Coffee – Brown Adventures

Coffee has been known in the West for just under 500 years, but coffee drinking was already widespread in the Arab world in the 13th century. There are many myths and amusing stories about the supposed origins of coffee. One thing that is agreed, however, is that its birthplace was in the province of Kaffa in Abyssinia; after all, the drink takes its name from this region. Coffee conquered the entire civilized world during the course of the 19th century.

The coffee we buy today is always a mixture of various types. Careful blending and roasting produces delicious and exclusive tastes. Coffee is drunk black, with milk or cream, and you can order a Café Mélange or a cappuccino, an expresso or an even stronger ristretto. There are many alternate ways of serving and enjoying coffee that go beyond the typical variations to be found in individual countries. It can be combined and refined with the most unlikely ingredients.

Coffee is highly esteemed by gourmets not only for its delicious taste but also for the invigorating effect of the caffeine. This primarily affects the central nervous system and produces a general mental alertness, increased receptivity, greater activity, and faster reactions. In earlier times, coffee beans were even used medicinally for their invigorating properties. Today, more and more people are choosing caffeine-free or less stimulating refined coffee that is "gentle on the stomach".

Oriental

1 tsp ground coffee
150 ml (6 fl.oz) hot water
½ tsp ground cardamom
sugar to taste

Brew the coffee with the ground cardamom. Sweeten to taste.

Café Glacier

1 tbsp ground coffee
100 ml (4 fl.oz) hot water
1 tsp candied orange peel
1 tsp ground hazelnuts
sugar to taste
3 tbsps cream

Brew the coffee. Blend the candied orange peel with 1 tbsp of cream and mix with the hazelnuts. Whip the remaining cream and mix all ingredients together.

Café Myrta

1 tbsp ground coffee
1 tbsp icing (confectioner's) sugar
1 tsp cocoa powder
150 ml (6 fl.oz) water
cream
vanilla sugar

Bring the coffee, sugar and cocoa almost to the boil. Strain into a cup. Lightly beat the cream and vanilla sugar and serve separately.

Choco Coffee

1 tsp ground coffee
50 ml (2 fl.oz) hot water
100 ml (4 fl.oz) hot chocolate
3 tbsps cream
vanilla sugar
some orange peel

Brew the coffee and pour into a cup with the chocolate. Beat the cream and vanilla sugar until stiff and top the drink with it. Grate the orange peel and sprinkle over the cream.

Café "Amandine"

150 ml (6 fl.oz) hot coffee
5 drops almond essence
1 tsp sugar
2 tbsps whipped cream
1 tsp candied fruit

Stir the almond essence and sugar into the coffee. Top with cream. Finely chop the candied fruit and sprinkle on the cream.

Café "Kaiser"

150 ml (6 fl.oz) hot coffee
1 egg yolk
sugar to taste
2 tbsps cream

Mix the egg yolk with ½ tsp of cold water. Add the cream and stir into the coffee. Sweeten.

 Oriental – Cafe Glacier – Cafe Myrta (in cup) – Chococafe

South America

1 heaped tsp instant coffee
1 tsp cocoa
75 ml (3 fl.oz) water
1 heaped tsp sugar
75 ml (3 fl.oz) milk
½ vanilla pod

Bring all the ingredients, except the vanilla, to the boil. Cut the vanilla pod in half, scrape it out and stir it into the hot drink.

Cinnamon Coffee

1 heaped tsp ground coffee
125 ml (5 fl.oz) water
a small piece of cinnamon stick
sugar to taste
4 grapes

Cut the cinnamon stick into four. Bring to the boil with the sugar and grapes and leave to stand for a while. Add coffee, bring to the boil and strain into a cup.

Spiced Coffee

1 tsp ground coffee
ground cardamom and nutmeg
50 ml (2 fl.oz) hot water
50 ml (2 fl.oz) whipping cream
½ tsp sugar
vanilla extract

Pour the water on to the coffee and spices and leave to stand for a while. Whip the cream, vanilla extract and sugar together and put into a cup. Sprinkle with the cardamom and pour the coffee over the top.

Cappuccino

50 ml (2 fl.oz) hot expresso coffee
50 ml (2 fl.oz) hot milk
2 tbsps cream
cocoa powder

Beat the milk until frothy. Pour into a cup with the coffee. Whip cream and use to top the drink. Sprinkle with cocoa powder.

Café "Gingembre"

1 tsp ground coffee
¼ tsp ground ginger
150 ml (6 fl.oz) hot water
1 tsp honey
cream

Mix the coffee and ground ginger together. Put the honey into a cup and pour on the coffee. Whip the cream and top the drink with it.

Coffcoa

100 ml (4 fl.oz) hot coffee
100 ml (4 fl.oz) hot cocoa
1 tsp candied sugar

Stir the cocoa, coffee and candied sugar together in a beaker.

Honey Sweet

1½ tsps ground coffee
125 ml (5 fl.oz) hot water
1 tbsp honey
whipping cream

Make the coffee. Let it stand for a while then filter it. Put the honey into a cup, pour on the coffee and garnish with whipped cream.

Cold Coffee

Coffee on the rocks

Perhaps we are not used to trying it like that, but that does not mean, by a long way, that cold coffee cannot taste delicious. In many countries it is "cool" to drink iced coffee. If you are in Italy and order a "caffe freddo", in Spain a "granizada de cafe" or an "iced coffee" in the U.S.A. then every waiter will know what you want and bring you an iced coffee. These drinks are particularly welcome in hot countries when the temperature rises because they are excellent thirst quenchers. You can make truly delicious drinks with cold coffee. The easiest way is to simply serve the chilled coffee on the rocks. Sometimes the coffee can also be semi-frozen and crushed before serving; then it will gradually thaw out completely. With a little imagination you can combine the cold coffee with various ingredients to produce delicious and refreshing drinks.
To make an iced coffee cocktail, you should always first leave the coffee to chill in the refrigerator (in a tightly-sealed container). Secondly, you should remember that for iced coffee drinks, the coffee needs to be twice as strong as usual. When the drink is chilled or frozen, or if ice cubes are added, it loses some of its strength. Properly prepared, however, cold coffee can preserve the full aroma of the beans.

Café a l'Orange

2 tsps ground coffee
100 ml (4 fl.oz) hot water
1 tsp sugar
2 tbsps crushed ice
4 slices of orange
a few drops of orange essence

Make the coffee and leave to stand for 1 minute. Filter, sweeten and let it cool. Put the orange slices, orange essence and ice into a glass. Top up with the coffee.

Full Power

30 ml (1 fl.oz) cold, sweetened
  coffee
90 ml (4 fl.oz) milk
½ tsp hazelnut purée
a few drops of lemon juice
crushed ice

Mix all the ingredients together and serve immediately.

Coffee Cup

100 ml (4 fl.oz) cold expresso
  coffee
1 tbsp chocolate powder
1 tsp sugar
50 ml (2 fl.oz) milk
2 tbsps whipped cream

Mix the chocolate, sugar and milk. Pour on the coffee and top with the whipped cream.

Ice Cream Coffee

100 ml (4 fl.oz) cold expresso
  coffee
1 scoop vanilla ice cream
2 tbsps cream
1 tbsp sugar
ice cubes

Mix the ingredients together. Serve with ice.

Cold Spiced Coffee

150 ml (6 fl.oz) hot expresso
  coffee
a small piece of vanilla pod
1 clove
1 tsp sugar
ice cubes
cream

Mix the expresso coffee with the spices and sugar. Leave to chill. Strain and pour over ice cubes. Serve with cream.

Coffee Flip

1 egg
50 ml (2 fl.oz) strong, sweetened
  coffee
ice cubes
nutmeg

Shake the ingredients (except the nutmeg). Pour into a glass and sprinkle with nutmeg.

Café a l'Orange – Full Power – Coffee Cup

Apricoff	*70 ml (3 fl.oz) cold coffee* *1 scoop vanilla ice cream* *50 ml (2 fl.oz) apricot juice* *30 ml (1 fl.oz) milk* *a few drops of almond essence*	Mix all the ingredients together and serve.
Colaco	*100 ml (4 fl.oz) cold, sweetened* *coffee* *2 tbsps cream* *ice cubes* *50 ml (2 fl.oz) cola*	Pour the coffee and cream over the ice. Stir well and top up with the cola.
Mocha Frost	*100 ml (4 fl.oz) cold expresso* *coffee* *1 tbsp liquid chocolate* *1 scoop coffee ice cream*	Mix all the ingredients together and serve immediately.

Cocoa and Chocolate

Culinary experiments with cocoa and chocolate

We have the American Indians to thank for the cocoa tree and its valued beans as we do for so many other important and useful plants. Cocoa and chocolate were sent forth into the whole world from Mexico and over the centuries have become a part of our culture. Today, of course, chocolate is particularly loved by children. In earlier times, however, cocoa products were so expensive that only the wealthy could afford to enjoy them. Even at the start of this century and after the two world wars cocoa and chocolate were delicacies reserved for special occasions.

In the meantime, cocoa and chocolate have secured a significant place for themselves in the food economy of the entire world. They are processed in many ways on an international scale and consumed with passion.

Drinking chocolate was the original way of enjoying cocoa for the American Indians. They used to season their brown brew with vanilla pods or honey. In the Caribbean, on the other hand, they still prefer to mix their cocoa with orange juice, and the latest trend is to add a scoop of vanilla ice cream to the drink. These examples show the multitude of ways of combining cocoa and chocolate with other ingredients and serve to encourage the gourmet on to further culinary experiments.

There are two qualities that all cocoa drinks share whether they are served hot or ice cold: they not only combine the pleasurable with the wholesome in a popular delicacy, but are also recognized as a quick source of energy.

Chocolate Power	*2 tbsps Ovaltine* *½ a lemon* *1 orange* *1 egg yolk* *2 tbsps sugar* *100 ml (4 fl.oz) milk* *25 ml (1 fl.oz) cream* *2 ice cubes*	Squeeze the orange and lemon. Mix with the other ingredients and serve immediately.
Blackcurrant Chocolate	*1 tbsp drinking chocolate powder* *200 ml (8 fl.oz) milk* *2 tbsps blackcurrant syrup* *ice cubes*	Whip the chocolate, milk and blackcurrant syrup together. Serve with ice.
Tennis Cup	*2 tbsps drinking chocolate* *powder* *1 egg* *1 tbsp candied ginger* *100 ml (4 fl.oz) milk* *lemon juice* *ice cubes*	Mix all the ingredients together.
Apple and Cinnamon Chocolate	*2 tbsps drinking chocolate* *powder* *½ an apple* *some lemon juice* *1 tbsp sugar* *150 ml (6 fl.oz) milk* *1 tsp cinnamon* *1 orange slice*	Peel, wash and slice the apple. Mix the drinking chocolate with the sliced apple, lemon juice, sugar, milk and cinnamon. Pour into a glass and chill. Garnish with a slice of orange.
Chocolate "Belle Helene"	*2 tbsps chocolate powder* *1 steamed pear, mashed* *1 tsp vanilla sugar* *200 ml (8 fl.oz) milk*	Mix all the ingredients together. Chill and serve.
Chocolate "Amandine"	*2 tbsps chocolate powder* *75 g (3 oz) marzipan* *200 ml (8 fl.oz) milk*	Mix all the ingredients together. Chill and serve.

Chocolate Power – Blackcurrant Chocolate – Tennis Cup

Chocolate Ginger

2 tbsps drinking chocolate
  powder
50 g (2 oz) candied ginger
200 ml (8 fl.oz) milk
sugar to taste
1 tbsp cream
brown sugar

Slice the ginger finely and leave to stand in the milk. Mix with the chocolate and sweeten to taste. Whip the cream until stiff and use to top the drink. Sprinkle with brown sugar.

Chocolate "Anna"

50 g (2 oz) grated chocolate
50 ml (2 fl.oz) cream
150 ml (6 fl.oz) milk
sugar to taste
a little orange peel

Whip the milk, cream and chocolate together and sweeten to taste. Pour into a glass and garnish with orange peel.

Drinking Chocolate

50 g (2 oz) dark chocolate
1 orange
½ a vanilla pod
150 ml (6 fl.oz) milk

Crumble the chocolate and melt. Grate a little orange peel and scrape out the vanilla pod. Add to the melted chocolate with the milk. Bring to the boil and serve.

Chocolate a l'Orange

2 tbsps chocolate powder
2 tbsps orange syrup
200 ml (8 fl.oz) milk
2 tbsps cream
candied orange peel

Mix the chocolate powder and orange syrup together. Whip the cream until stiff and use to top the drink. Chop the candied orange peel very finely and sprinkle over the top.

Chocolate Tornado

1 tbsp instant cocoa
1 orange
2 tbsps sugar
2 tbsps blackcurrant purée
2 tbsps yogurt
125 ml (5 fl.oz) milk

Squeeze the orange and mix together with the other ingredients.

Chocolate "Marathon"

3 tbsps liquid chocolate
200 ml (8 fl.oz) milk
1 tsp instant coffee
sugar

Heat the chocolate, milk and coffee, but do not boil. Sweeten with sugar and serve.

Choco Mint Shake

600 ml (20 fl.oz) chilled milk
4-8 drops peppermint essence
4 tbsps chocolate ice cream
50 g (2 oz) shredded chocolate

Blend the peppermint essence with the milk. Add the chocolate ice cream and blend until smooth. Pour into four glasses and sprinkle with grated chocolate. Serve immediately.

1 tbsp chocolate vermicelli 1 egg yolk: some orange peel 150 ml (6 fl.oz) milk 1 ice cube vanilla sugar 2 tbsps cream	Mix the orange peel, vermicelli, egg yolk, milk and ice cube together. Season with vanilla sugar and chill. Whip the cream until stiff and use to top the drink.	**Chocolate Flip**
50 g (2 oz) liquid chocolate 150 ml (6 fl.oz) milk sugar to taste 1 scoop vanilla ice cream 2 tbsps whipping cream	Mix the chocolate and milk together. Sweeten to taste and chill. Put the vanilla ice cream into a tall glass and fill up with the chocolate milk. Whip the cream until stiff and use to top the drink.	**Chocolate Revel**
2 tbsps chocolate drinking powder 1 tbsp apricot jam sugar to taste 125 ml (5 fl.oz) milk 2 tbsps low fat curd cheese 1 tsp lemon juice 1 ice cube	Mix all the ingredients together and serve immediately.	**Chocolate Apricot**

2 tbsps drinking chocolate
  powder
1 tsp cinnamon
1 pinch each ground cloves
  and ginger
1 tbsp sugar
200 ml (8 fl.oz) milk
	Shake the ingredients well. Can also be drunk warm.	**Chocolate Spice**

2 tbsps chocolate powder ½ a banana 1 egg yolk 1 scoop vanilla ice cream 100 ml (4 fl.oz) milk	Mix all the ingredients together. Chill and serve.	**Slalom Flip**
2 tbsps chocolate powder 1 tsp instant coffee 1 tsp sugar 200 ml (8 fl.oz) milk 2 tbsps cream	Shake the ingredients well and serve immediately.	**Fifty-Fifty**

Chilled Chocolate Cream	2 heaped tbsps drinking chocolate 3 tbsps boiling water 900 ml (30 fl.oz) chilled milk 1 tsp vanilla essence 2 tbsps whipped cream 4 tbsps shredded chocolate	Mix the drinking chocolate with the water and whip together with milk and vanilla essence. Pour into four glasses and decorate with cream and shredded chocolate.
Chocolate Shake	2 heaped tbsps drinking chocolate 3 tbsps boiling water 900 ml (30 fl.oz) chilled milk 4 heaped tbsps vanilla ice cream	Mix the drinking chocolate with the boiling water and whip with milk and two tablespoons of ice cream. Divide the remaining ice cream between four glasses. Pour on milk mixture and serve immediately.
Chocolate Cream Special	100 g (4 oz) dark chocolate ½ tsp ground cinnamon 600 ml (20 fl.oz) milk 150 ml (6 fl.oz) whipping cream	Put the milk into a saucepan. Add the chocolate and cinnamon and heat gently until dissolved. Bring to the boil. Whip the cream and whip most of it into the milk. Pour into four glasses and top with remaining whipped cream and cinnamon or grated chocolate.
Brazilian Banana Milkshake	600 ml (20 fl.oz) chilled milk 3 tbsps drinking chocolate 150 g (5 oz) natural yogurt 1 mashed banana chopped walnuts	Whip all the ingredients together until smooth. Pour into four glasses and top with chopped walnuts.

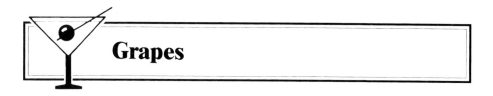

Grapes

Energy and vitality with grape juice

The juice of a fine grape is particularly refreshing and stimulating when served chilled. Its energy goes straight into the bloodstream. Even as an aperitif it will set the mood. With a glass of alcohol-free grape juice you can drink a double toast to your health. To add variety to health, grape juice can be mixed in many different ways.
Pleasure and health are combined in all grape juice drinks.

Red Grenadier	100 ml (4 fl.oz) red grape juice 20 ml (⅔ fl.oz) grenadine syrup 70 ml (2½ fl.oz) apricot juice ice cubes	Mix the grape juice, grenadine and apricot juice. Serve with ice.
Pick-me-up	120 ml (5 fl.oz) white grape juice 1 peach 30 ml (1 fl.oz) strawberry syrup	Quarter the peach, prick with a fork and put in a glass. Top up with strawberry syrup and grape juice. Stir well and serve with a bar spoon.
Vanilla Party	150 ml (6 fl.oz) sparkling grape juice 30 g (1 oz) blackberries 4 drops vanilla essence ice cubes	Mix the blackberries, vanilla essence and grape juice. Serve with ice.
Oranut	100 ml (4 fl.oz) sparkling grape juice 50 ml (2 fl.oz) pineapple juice juice of 1 orange crushed ice	Mix the juices well and serve with ice.
Tomeg	150 ml (6 fl.oz) grape spritzer 50 ml (2 fl.oz) tomato juice a pinch of nutmeg Worcester sauce	Mix everything well and serve chilled.
Ruby Red	150 ml (6 fl.oz) red grape juice 2 tbsps curd cheese 40 g (2 oz) blackberries sugar to taste	Mix the ingredients. Sweeten to taste and serve.
Honeymoon	100 ml (4 fl.oz) white grape juice ½ a sliced apple 1 tsp grated hazelnuts 50 ml (2 fl.oz) apple juice 25 g (1 oz) raspberries	Mix all the ingredients, except the raspberries, together. Put the raspberries into a glass and top up with the liquid.

100 ml (4 fl.oz) white grape juice *⅛ of a melon* *2 tsps lemon juice* *1 tsp cane sugar*	Mix all the ingredients together. Sweeten to taste and serve.	**Melon Grape Mix**
100 ml (4 fl.oz) white grape juice *1 scoop vanilla ice cream* *½ a small, ripe banana* *1 lemon, juice and rind*	Mix all the ingredients together.	**Banana Grape**
150 ml (6 fl.oz) white grape juice *50 ml (2 fl.oz) celery juice* *pepper, salt* *celery leaves*	Mix the celery and grape juice. Season. Garnish with celery leaves.	**Celery Mix**
120 ml (5 fl.oz) white or red *grape juice* *50 ml (2 fl.oz) pineapple juice* *20 ml (⅔ fl.oz) lemon juice* *ice cubes*	Mix the juices. Pour into a glass and serve with ice.	**Greetings from the South**
150 ml (6 fl.oz) red grape juice *2 tbsps natural yogurt* *20 g (1 oz) redcurrants*	Beat the grape juice and yogurt. Remove stalks from redcurrants, put into a glass and pour on the liquid. Variation: mix all the ingredients together and sweeten.	**Red Wonder**
100 ml (4 fl.oz) white grape juice *1 tsp each strawberry and* *raspberry syrup* *1 tsp lemon juice* *50 ml (2 fl.oz) orange juice* *ice cubes*	Shake all the ingredients briefly and serve.	**Tutti Frutti Cocktail**
100 ml (4 fl.oz) white grape juice *50 ml (2 fl.oz) pineapple juice* *50 ml (2 fl.oz) blackcurrant juice* *ice cubes* *peppermint leaves*	Mix the juices and add ice. Garnish with peppermint leaves.	**"Merano" Refresher**

*Red Grenadier – Pick-me-up – Vanilla Party – Oranut –
Tomeg*

100 ml (4 fl.oz) white grape juice *juice of ½ a lemon* *1 tbsp sugar* *50 ml (2 fl.oz) mineral water* *1 tsp honey* *½ an egg white*	Mix all the ingredients until the mixture is thick and frothy.	**Grand Elysee**
100 ml (4 fl.oz) white grape juice *juice of ½ a lemon* *100 ml (4 fl.oz) ginger ale* *a slice of orange* *peppermint leaves*	Mix the grape juice with the lemon juice and ginger ale. Garnish the rim of the glass with the slice of orange and peppermint leaves.	**Brasiliana**
100 ml (4 fl.oz) white grape juice *50 ml (2 fl.oz) each lemon and* *orange juice* *a pinch of cinnamon* *2 leaves fresh peppermint* *crushed ice*	Mix together the juices with the chopped peppermint, cinnamon and ice.	**Gramon**
100 ml (4 fl.oz) white grape juice *70 ml (3 fl.oz) apple juice* *1 tbsp lemon juice* *ground ginger* *ice cubes*	Mix the juices. Season and serve chilled.	**Grapple**
150 ml (6 fl.oz) red grape juice *juice of ½ a lemon* *1 tsp thick pear juice* *1 tbsp .whipped cream*	Mix everything together well and top with cream.	**Red Pear**
100 ml (4 fl.oz) grape spritzer *¼ of a cucumber* *dill tips* *a little lemon juice* *mixed spices* *ice cubes*	Press the cucumber. Mix with the dill tips and ice cubes. Top up with grape spritzer and season with lemon juice and mixed spices.	**Dillgrape**

Parspri	150 ml (6 fl.oz) grape spritzer ½ bunch of parsley juice of ½ a lemon	Mix the parsley and grape spritzer. Strain and stir in the lemon juice.
Jafgra	150 ml (6 fl.oz) sparkling grape juice 4 slices each grapefruit and orange 1 tsp lemon juice ice cubes	Peel the fruit slices and mix with lemon juice and ice cubes. Top up with grape juice.
Party Mix	50 ml (2 fl.oz) sparkling grape juice 50 ml (2 fl.oz) pear juice a slice of pineapple 1 ice cube	Mix all the ingredients together.
Gralem	100 ml (4 fl.oz) sparkling grape juice ½ an apple, peeled 1 scoop lemon ice cream 1 tbsp blackcurrant juice lemon juice if desired	Finely dice the apple and put into a glass with the lemon ice cream. Top up with blackcurrant and grape juice. Season with lemon juice, if desired.
Party Berry Punch	2 bottles sparkling grape juice 500 ml (20 fl.oz) mineral water 15 g (1 oz) each blackberries, raspberries and redcurrants (or fruits in season) 2 grapefruits 4 tbsps honey a few fresh peppermint leaves ice cubes	Press the grapefruits. Gently heat the juice and dissolve the honey in it. Mix with the mineral water. Wash the berries and add them along with peppermint leaves. Leave to stand for 30 minutes. Top up with sparkling grape juice and serve with ice.

Pipped and Stone Fruits

Pipped and stone fruits fresh from the press

Fruit should not be enjoyed just now and again when the occasion arises, it should be a fixed part of your daily menu. It is one of the indispensable corner stones of a healthy diet as it provides the body with essential minerals, trace elements and vitamins. How about trying a fruit juice as an aperitif or just between meals?

Alongside the processed juices on sale throughout the year, there are also the fresh home-pressed apple, pear and grape juices available at harvest times. At home, with the aid of a food processor, you can press your stocks of apples and pears the whole year through. We could take a leaf out of the farmers' book and mix different proportions of these two fruits. The taste of these pressed juices will depend on which variety of fruit is used. The juices of freshly pressed cherries, grapes, plums and apricots are also delicious. Make use of harvest time and get those juices flowing.

Pear and Cranberry	*125 ml (5 fl. oz) pear juice* *1 tsp lemon juice* *½ tbsp cranberries* *ice cubes*	Shake everything together well and serve chilled.
Apple and Blood Orange Juice	*150 ml (6 fl. oz) apple juice* *50 ml (2 fl. oz) blood orange juice* *2 leaves lemon balm* *ice cubes*	Chop the lemon balm finely. Whip well with the juices and serve with ice.
Sour Grapes	*350 g (12 oz) grapes, de-stalked* *50 ml (2 fl. oz) lemon juice* *1 tsp honey* *½ bunch parsley*	Press the parsley and grapes and mix with the honey and lemon juice. Shake it all together well and serve immediately.
Honey Plum	*80 ml (3 fl. oz) plum juice* *1 small egg* *1 tsp honey* *1 ice cube* *apple juice*	Shake everything together well and top up with apple juice.
Pineapricot	*80 ml (3 fl. oz) apricot juice* *25 ml (1 fl. oz) pineapple juice* *1 apricot* *2 cherries* *crushed ice*	Mix everything together well and serve chilled.
Applecocoa	*200 ml (8 fl. oz) apple juice* *1 tbsp cold instant cocoa powder* *1 pinch cinnamon* *sugar to taste*	Beat the apple juice, cocoa powder and cinnamon together. Sweeten to taste.
Apple and Celery Juice	*200 g (7 oz) apples* *50 ml (2 fl. oz) celery juice* *1 tbsp lemon juice*	Blend the apples and mix together with the celery and lemon juice.

Pear and Cranberry – Apple and Blood Orange Juice –
Sour Grapes – Honey Plum – Pineapricot

Pearon	100 ml (4 fl.oz) pear juice 1 scoop lemon ice cream a pinch of cinnamon mineral water ice cubes	Mix everything together well. Top up with mineral water and serve with ice.
Peamon	2 pears juice of 1 lemon ½ tsp thick pear juice	Press the pears. Shake well with the lemon and pear juice.
Apple and Horseradish Juice	350 g (12 oz) apples 1 cm (½″) piece of horseradish a little salt	Peel the horseradish and blend with the apples. Mix well and add a little salt.
Bitter Apple	120 ml (5 fl.oz) apple juice 2 tbsps orange juice grated lemon peel 1-2 drops angostura bitters mineral water	Mix the orange juice, lemon peel and angostura bitters together. Add to the apple juice, beat together well and add some mineral water.
Leplum	80 ml (3 fl.oz) plum juice 1 scoop lemon ice cream a pinch of cinnamon mineral water	Shake everything together and top up with mineral water.
Spiced Plum	100 ml (4 fl.oz) plum juice 20 ml (1 fl.oz) grapefruit syrup a pinch of ground cloves ice cubes mineral water	Shake everything together and top up with mineral water.
Candied Cream Plum	120 ml (5 fl.oz) plum juice ½ tsp candied cherries 40 ml (1½ fl.oz) whipping cream ice cubes	Mix everything together well and serve chilled.

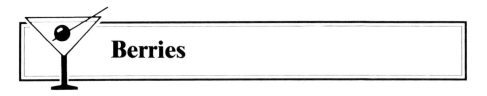

Berries

Berry cocktails, as bright as lanterns

The intense brightness of fresh berry cocktails is matched only by their taste. However, it is essential to use only the juice of fully-ripened fruits. Depending on the sugar content and taste of the berries you will produce a more or a less sweet juice or a slightly sour one. Even the place where the berries ripen and the time they are picked while ripening can cause differences in taste among berries of the same type. Different kinds of berries can also be combined beautifully with one another. A variety of ingredients can refine the drink without it losing the dominant fruity aroma of the berries themselves.

As only the taste of the berries is important when producing juices it is possible to use over-ripe berries in summer. In season it makes sense to make the most of special offers and to go out and pick the berries in your garden and in the woods. Any left over berries that cannot be used at the time can easily be frozen so that a few months later – in the middle of winter – you can produce those berry juices so rich in vitamins. At that time of year, when the range of fruit on the market is somewhat reduced, berry drinks are especially welcome.

Orberry	80 g (3 oz) strawberries 100 ml (4 fl.oz) orange juice 1 tsp vanilla sugar	Mix the strawberries and orange juice with sugar.
Cherrypear	250 g (9 oz) cherries 100 g (4 oz) pears a little sugar ice cubes	Press the cherries and pears. Lightly sweeten and serve with ice.
Cherramon	100 ml (4 fl.oz) cherry juice 50 ml (2 fl.oz) apple juice raw cherries a pinch of cinnamon ice cubes	Mix the cherries, juices and cinnamon together. Serve with ice.
Strawberry and Cranberry	80 ml (3 fl.oz) strawberry juice 40 ml (1½ fl.oz) orange juice 1 small scoop vanilla ice cream ½ tsp cranberries	Shake all the ingredients well together.
Strawberroney	80 ml (3 fl.oz) strawberry juice 4 tbsps each orange and lemon juice 1 tsp honey crushed ice	Shake everything together well and serve cold.
Lemberry	100 ml (4 fl.oz) raspberry juice 3 tbsps each lemon and orange juice crushed ice	Shake everything together well and serve cold.
Raspberry Choc	100 g (4 oz) raspberries 1½ tbsps sugar 1½ tbsps cocoa powder 100 ml (4 fl.oz) milk ½ vanilla pod	Mix the raspberries, cocoa and sugar with the milk. Scrape out the vanilla, add to the mixture and stir well. Serve with ice.

Orberry – Cherry Pear – Cherramon

Bilcarro	*80 ml (3 fl.oz) bilberry juice* *40 ml (1½ fl.oz) carrot juice* *lemon mineral water* *ice cubes*	Stir the juices together and top up with mineral water. Serve with ice.
Blackana	*80 ml (3 fl.oz) blackberry juice* *50 ml (2 fl.oz) pineapple juice* *50 ml (2 fl.oz) grape juice* *fresh peppermint leaves, chopped* *ice cubes*	Shake everything well together.
Repear	*80 ml (3 fl.oz) redcurrant juice* *50 ml (2 fl.oz) pear juice* *a little grapefruit juice* *ice cubes*	Mix everything together well and top up with grapefruit juice.
Elgin	*80 ml (3 fl.oz) elderberry juice* *1 tbsp lemon juice* *ginger ale* *crushed ice*	Mix everything together well. Serve chilled.
Raspli	*100 ml (4 fl.oz) raspberry juice* *1 tbsp lime juice* *bitter lemon* *ice cubes*	Mix the juices well together. Add ice cubes and top up with bitter lemon.
Cherry Vanilla	*100 ml (4 fl.oz) cherry juice* *1 scoop vanilla ice cream* *mineral water* *1 ice cube*	Shake together the cherry juice and vanilla ice cream. Top up with mineral water and add the ice cube.
Vitalim	*150 ml (6 fl.oz) blackcurrant juice* *1 tbsp lime juice* *1 tbsp maple syrup* *ice cubes*	Mix everything together well and serve with ice.
Cherry Cola	*80 ml (3 fl.oz) cherry juice* *40 ml (1½ fl.oz) milk* *1 ice cube* *Coca-Cola*	Mix everything together well and top up with Coca-Cola.

Bilcarro – Blackana – Repear – Elgin – Raspli

Bilcream	350g (12 oz) bilberries 1 tbsp lemon juice 2 tbsps cream 1 tbsp sugar	Press the bilberries and mix well with the other ingredients.
Billemon	120 ml (5 fl.oz) bilberry juice 2 small scoops lemon sorbet	Shake the bilberry juice and sorbet together well.
Blackora	80 g (3 oz) blackberries 50 ml (2 fl.oz) orange juice 1 ice cube ginger ale	Mix everything together well and top up with ginger ale.
Blackream	100 ml (4 fl.oz) blackberry juice 2 tbsps cream a little nutmeg and ground cloves lemon mineral water	Shake everything together well.
Limelder	125 ml (5 fl.oz) elderberry juice juice of 1 lime mineral water ice cubes	Mix everything together well. Serve chilled.
Eldenilla	80 ml (3 fl.oz) elderberry juice 1 scoop vanilla ice cream a little cinnamon lemon mineral water	Mix the vanilla ice cream, elderberry juice and cinnamon together. Pour into glasses and top up with mineral water.
Raspberry Surprise	75 g (3 oz) raspberries 100 ml (4 fl.oz) pasteurized milk 1 tsp sugar ½ tbsp lemon juice a pinch of salt	Mix everything together well and serve immediately.
Berry Berry	120 g (4 oz) each redcurrants and blackcurrants ½ of a banana crushed ice	Press the berries and mix with the banana. Shake with crushed ice.

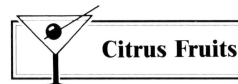

Citrus Fruits

Citrus fruits – the powerful juice dispensers

Orange or grapefruit juice at breakfast is refreshing and extremely invigorating at an early hour. The high vitamin and mineral content found in citrus fruits supplies us with vitality and energy. There are many other times throughout the day when you can enjoy these light fruit juices, be it as an aperitif, with your meal or as a healthy snack.

Juicy citrus fruits are available all year round. A fruit press will enable you to make fruity and strong tasting drinks both quickly and easily. As citrus fruits contain acids, like all other fruits and vegetables, you should not use any containers or equipment made of metal or copper when making fruit juice. This will avoid both damaging the taste and causing discoloration of the juice. The juice will taste just as pure and natural as the fruit itself.

Without a doubt, the orange is our most popular citrus fruit. Both it and the grapefruit are especially suitable for trying out with various ingredients to create original drinks. You can produce combinations that perhaps at first sight appear somewhat unusual, but whose culinary value is accordingly higher. You can also mix exquisite drinks based on lemon juice which are particularly good for quenching the thirst on hot days. Many drinks can also be improved by adding just a few drops of lemon juice.

Oraberry	100 ml (4 fl.oz) orange juice 25 ml (1 fl.oz) lemon juice 3 strawberries a little grated orange peel 1 tsp sugar ice cubes	Mix everything together well and serve with ice.
Nordic Grapefruit Juice	100 ml (4 fl.oz) grapefruit juice 100 ml (4 fl.oz) redcurrant juice a pinch of ground cloves a pinch of ground cinnamon sugar to taste	Mix everything together well. Serve without ice and not too chilled.
Lemolim	1 lemon and 1 lime 3 drops vanilla extract a little artificial sweetener mineral water ice cubes	Press the citrus fruits. Season with the vanilla and sweetener and serve chilled.
Orange and Tomato Juice	100 ml (4 fl.oz) orange juice 50 ml (2 fl.oz) tomato juice ½ tbsp lemon juice a little Worcester sauce a drop of Tabasco sauce 1 ice cube	Mix the juices well together. Pour over the ice cubes, season and stir.
Orange and Apple Juice	50 ml (2 fl.oz) orange juice 50 ml (2 fl.oz) apple juice ½ scoop orange ice cream ice cubes prepared cubes of orange	Mix the juices and the orange ice cream. Pour on to the ice cubes and add the cubes of orange.
Orange Citrus	150 ml (6 fl.oz) orange juice 50 ml (2 fl.oz) lemon juice 1 tsp honey nutmeg	Dissolve the honey in the lemon juice and mix well with the orange juice and a pinch of nutmeg.
Grapfle	100 ml (4 fl.oz) grapefruit juice 80 ml (3 fl.oz) apple juice ice cubes	Mix everything together well and serve with ice cubes.

Oraberry – Nordic Grapefruit Juice – Lemolim

Legrap

75 ml (3 fl.oz) lemon juice
50 ml (2 fl.oz) grape juice
50 ml (2 fl.oz) pineapple juice
crushed ice

Mix all the juices well together and serve chilled.

Orango

80 ml (3 fl.oz) orange juice
¼ of a mango
20 g (1 oz) lemon syrup
mineral water
ice cubes

Mix the orange juice and mango. Mix in the syrup, top up with mineral water and serve chilled.

Orange Shake

100 ml (4 fl.oz) orange juice
75 g (3 oz) sour cream
1 tsp sugar
½ tsp vanilla sugar

Mix everything together well.

Caramo

150 ml (6 fl.oz) orange juice
1 tbsp sugar
crushed ice

Brown the sugar, add the orange juice and serve with crushed ice.

Citrus fruits are rich in vitamin C and low in calories *

per 100 g:	Vitamin A (mg)	Vitamin C (mg)	kcal	kJ
Orange	15	50	53	222
Orange juice (freshly pressed)	12	52	47	197
Grapefruit	3	41	43	180
Grapefruit juice	traces	40	39	163
Lemon	3 .	53	38	159
Lemon juice	2	51	35	146
Daily vitamin need	0.9 mg	70-75 mg		

Important minerals in oranges, grapefruits and lemons are: potassium, calcium and phosphorous.

* Hans Scherz, *The Great Nutrition Table*, Munich 1982

Exotic Fruits

Exotic cocktails – tropical atmosphere in a glass

The cocktails we got to know in exotic climes can still carry us away at home. Almost daily, fruits are brought in from foreign lands on planes and refrigerator ships. Recently, our long familiar oranges, bananas and pineapples have been joined by kiwi fruit, mangoes, papayas and many other fruit delicacies from the tropics.

Exotic fruits are noted for their versatility. They harmonize with the most diverse fruits, berries and liquids and can be exquisitely combined with many other ingredients. They can also be enjoyed in very different ways. No wonder that drinks made with exotic fruits taste excellent and remind us of time spent in foreign countries.

Some exotic fruits are notable for their vitamin and nutrient content. The kiwi fruit is more or less a "vitamin bomb". One single fruit can easily satisfy an adult's entire daily vitamin C requirement.

Peaches, pineapples, mangoes, papayas and, to a lesser extent, honeydew melons, contain considerable amounts of vitamins and minerals. The banana, however, easily leads the field in the variety and balance of its individual nutrients. It contains eleven vitamins, the most important being A and E.

Exotic fruit cocktails with their southern magic are an attractive treat and a refreshing change for your palate.

Pinemon Juice

100 ml (4 fl.oz) pineapple juice
1 tbsp lemon juice
2 tsps sugar
50 ml (2 fl.oz) apple juice
ice cubes

Mix everything together well and serve chilled.

Banavan

½ of a banana
½ scoop vanilla ice cream
100 ml (4 fl.oz) apple juice
ice cubes

Mix everything well and serve chilled.

Melurrant

150 g (5 oz) watermelon
20 g (1 oz) redcurrant syrup
1 tsp lemon juice
2-3 drops vanilla extract
ice cubes

Mix everything well and serve with ice.

Peach and Rhubarb Juice

150 g (5 oz) peaches
1 stick rhubarb
2-3 drops vanilla essence
2 ice cubes

Press the rhubarb and peaches. Add vanilla essence and serve with ice.

Peach Delight

2 half peaches
50 g (2 oz) sugar
½ cinnamon pod
1 clove
1 tbsp lemon juice
100 ml (4 fl.oz) water
½ of a banana
50 ml (2 fl.oz) apple juice

Peel the peach, cube and simmer for 4 minutes in water with the sugar, cinnamon, clove and lemon juice. Leave to cool. Remove the spices, add the banana, mix and add apple juice.

Pineapple Tea

1 slice of pineapple
100 ml (4 fl.oz) black tea
½ tbsp lemon juice
sugar to taste
50 ml (2 fl.oz) mineral water

Mix the pineapple with cold tea and lemon juice. Sweeten and pour on mineral water.

Pinemon Juice – Banavan – Melurrant –
Peach and Rhubarb Juice

Papache
80 ml (3 fl.oz) papaya juice
80 ml (3 fl.oz) cherry juice
1 pinch each of nutmeg and
    ground ginger
ice cubes

Mix the juices together well. Season and serve chilled.

Mangole
80 ml (3 fl.oz) mango juice
1 scoop lemon sorbet
a little sugar
1 tbsp crushed ice
milk

Shake everything together well and top up with milk.

Melon Juice
½ of a honeydew melon
2½ tbsps lime juice
red grape juice
ice cubes

Press the melon, mix with lime juice and top up with grape juice.

Kiwit
1 kiwi fruit
1 tbsp lemon juice
bitter lemon
crushed ice cubes

Mix the kiwi fruit with lemon juice and ice. Top up with bitter lemon.

Banaho
½ of a banana
1 egg
½ tbsp honey
100 ml (4 fl.oz) milk

Beat the egg, mash the banana and mix well with the honey and milk. Serve cold.

Banora
½ of a banana
50 ml (2 fl.oz) orange juice
½ tsp vanilla sugar
lemon mineral water

Mix everything well. Top up with mineral water.

Pincoff
100 ml (4 fl.oz) pineapple juice
40 ml (1½ fl.oz) apple juice
40 ml (1½ fl.oz) coffee cream
ice cubes

Mix the pineapple and apple juices. Add cream and shake well. Serve with ice.

1 banana *60 g (2 oz) bilberries* *a pinch of cinnamon* *a little sugar* *mineral water*	Mix everything well. Season and top up with mineral water.	**Banana Bill**
40 ml (1½ fl.oz) pineapple juice *20 ml (⅔ fl.oz) orange juice* *2 tsps sugar* *mineral water*	Mix everything well. Top up with mineral water and serve with ice.	**Pinissimo**
100 ml (4 fl.oz) pineapple juice *100 ml (4 fl.oz) tomato juice* *1 small pinch salt* *1 ice cube*	Put all the ingredients into a shaker. Shake well and serve immediately.	**Pineapple and Tomato Juice**
100 ml (4 fl.oz) pineapple juice *50 ml (2 fl.oz) lemon juice* *50 ml (2 fl.oz) cream* *ice cubes*	Shake well with ice, strain and serve.	**Pineapple Cocktail**
100 ml (4 fl.oz) pineapple juice *¼ of a slice of pineapple* *2 tbsps drinking chocolate* * powder* *100 ml (4 fl.oz) milk* *a little lemon juice*	Mix everything together well. Serve immediately.	**Pineapple Choc**
100 ml (4 fl.oz) peach juice *50 ml (2 fl.oz) grapefruit juice* *a pinch of cinnamon* *ginger ale* *ice cubes*	Shake everything well and top up with ginger ale.	**Peacafruit**
150 g (5 oz) peaches *1 tbsp lemon juice* *1 tbsp sugar* *1 egg white* *crushed ice*	Press the peach and mix well with the other ingredients. Serve with crushed ice.	**Snowpeach**

Papache – Mangole – Melon Juice – Kiwit

Vegetables

Vegetable juice in a cocktail glass

Raw vegetables, served as a refreshing cocktail, are rich in minerals, and ideal as an aperitif or even in place of soup. Anybody who turns up their nose at the idea, believing that vegetable juices may well be healthy, but are no fun for the palate, should try a freshly-pressed juice soon. They will most certainly change their mind. In the right combination, pressed and well-seasoned vegetable juices taste excellent. Home-made juices are so tasty that we will soon not want to do without them.

You can usually tell the difference between a freshly-pressed vegetable juice and a good, preservable, commercially-available product instantly. The homemade juice will be different every time depending on the taste of the vegetable used. If, for example, the carrots used for pressing are a little sweet or the asparagus a little bitter then the juice will also share this characteristic. That is why, when making juice, it is worth choosing first class vegetables and to make sure that they are washed thoroughly. Thanks to modern electrical juice extractors, it is possible to produce your own juices from practically any vegetable without much fuss.

Pea Cocktail

150g (5 oz) peas
½ bunch parsley
1 carrot
2 mushrooms
1 ice cube

Press everything, mix well and serve chilled.

Beetrive

100 ml (4 fl.oz) beetroot juice
2 Belgian endives
1 tsp chopped chives

Prepare and press the endives. Mix well with beetroot juice and chives.

Caulrabi Juice

200 g (7 oz) cauliflower
150 g (5 oz) kohlrabi
1 tsp thick pear juice
1 tsp lemon juice
a pinch of ginger

Press the vegetables, mix well with the pear juice and lemon juice and season.

Radiro

150 g (5 oz) radishes
80 g (3 oz) carrots
fresh thyme
salt
ice cubes

Press the radishes and carrots. Season with finely chopped thyme and salt. Serve with ice.

Asparato

250 g (9 oz) asparagus
1 potato
½ tbsp chopped parsley
salt, pepper

Peel the asparagus and press with the potato. Season and stir in the parsley.

Red Honey

200 g (7 oz) red cabbage
1 apple
3 tsps each lemon and
   orange juice
1 tsp honey
1 tsp cream
1 ice cube

Press the red cabbage and apple. Squeeze the lemon and orange juice. Mix everything with the remaining ingredients.

Sour Tomato

50 ml (2 fl.oz) sauerkraut juice
175 ml (7 fl.oz) tomato juice
1 tsp lemon juice
salt, pepper, Worcester sauce
ice cubes

Shake everything well. Season and serve with ice.

¼ of a green pepper ¼ of an onion 1 celery stalk ¼ of a cucumber 1 tsp lemon juice ice cubes	Press the vegetables, mix well and serve with ice.	**Harvest Cup**
100 g (4 oz) fennel 100 ml (4 fl.oz) milk sugar ginger ale	Press the fennel. Shake it with the milk and sugar. Top up with ginger ale.	**Fennel Ale**
a bunch of parsley 300 g (10 oz) grapes 2 tbsps lemon juice 1 tbsp honey	Press the parsley and grapes. Mix well with the honey and lemon juice.	**Parwhite**
100 g (4 oz) kohlrabi 250 g (9 oz) melon 4 leaves lemon balm 1 tbsp lemon juice a pinch of salt	Press the kohlrabi, melon and lemon balm. Season with the lemon juice and salt.	**Kohlon**
300 g (10 oz) radish 1 apple ⅛ of an onion ½ tbsp lemon juice a little salt and water	Blend the radish, apple and onion. Mix well and season.	**Radish and Apple Cocktail**
40 g (2 oz) radish and cucumber 60 g (2½ oz) carrots chives a small piece of a pepper sweet paprika 2 ice cubes	Press the vegetables and mix with the pepper. Season. Serve with ice and garnish with chives.	**Radish and Paprika Cocktail**

Nucarro	150 ml (6 fl. oz) carrot juice 1 tbsp each lemon and orange juice 2 tbsps whipped cream nutmeg, ginger, sugar ice cubes	Mix the juices well. Season. Fold in the cream and serve with ice.
Tomato and Spinach Juice	100 ml (4 fl. oz) tomato juice 160 g (5 oz) fresh spinach leaves 2 basil leaves a little salt	Wash the spinach and form into balls. Blend with the basil leaves. Mix with tomato juice.
Tomato Juice a l'Italienne	150 ml (6 fl. oz) tomato juice 1 basil leaf a little salt garlic powder	Season the tomato juice well. Chop the basil finely. Mix everything together well.
Cucumber and Rhubarb Juice	⅓ of a cucumber 250 g (9 oz) rhubarb 1½ tsps thick pear juice	Blend the cucumber and rhubarb. Mix with thick pear juice and shake well.
Beetroot and Lemon	200 ml (8 fl. oz) beetroot juice 1 tsp thick pear juice 1 tsp lemon juice 2 ice cubes	Crush the ice slightly and beat it well in with the beetroot juice, the lemon juice and the pear juice.
Tangy Tomato Juice	100 ml (4 fl. oz) tomato juice 50 ml (2 fl. oz) grapefruit juice ½ tbsp lemon juice salt, a little nutmeg 1-2 drops Tabasco sauce a little Worcester sauce	Stir all the ingredients well together. Season to make a tangy taste.
Tomato and Orange Juice	100 ml (4 fl. oz) tomato juice 70 ml (2½ fl. oz) orange juice a little salt ice cubes	Shake the juices well. Lightly salt and serve with ice.

Pea Cocktail – Beetrive – Caulrabi Juice – Radiro –
Asparato

Careami	100 ml (4 fl. oz) carrot juice 4 tbsps cream 2 tbsps milk ground rosemary, sugar ice cubes	Shake everything together well. Season and serve with ice.
Caroberry	100 ml (4 fl. oz) carrot juice 50 ml (2 fl. oz) cream ½ tbsp grapes 1 tsp vanilla sugar	Chop the grapes and shake together with the other ingredients.
Micarro	60 ml (2 fl. oz) carrot juice 80 ml (3 fl. oz) pasteurized milk 50 ml (2 fl. oz) mineral water 1 tsp lemon juice 1 tbsp sugar	Shake the juices and milk and sugar. Top up with the mineral water.
Carrotom	140 g (5 oz) carrots 120 g (4 oz) tomatoes ½ tsp lemon juice a pinch each of mustard powder, salt, mixed spices ice cubes	Press the carrots and tomatoes. Add the lemon juice, season and serve with ice.
Carromom Juice	250 g (9 oz) carrots 150 g (5 oz) apples ⅛ of a cucumber a pinch of cardamom	Blend the vegetables and apples and season with cardamom.
Carroley Juice	250 g (9 oz) carrots 150 g (5 oz) celery ½ bunch parsley	Wash everything well. Blend, mix well and serve with an ice cube.
Cucumber and Pumpkin Juice	¼ of a cucumber 100 g (4 oz) pumpkin, prepared ½ tbsp lemon juice	Peel the cucumber and blend with the pumpkin. Add the lemon juice and mix well.

75 ml (3 fl.oz) radish juice *100 ml (4 fl.oz) pasteurized milk*	Shake everything well. Season and serve with ice.	**Radmilk**
200 g (7 oz) white cabbage *½ of a carrot* *sea salt* *freshly-milled pepper* *ice cubes*	Press the carrot and the cabbage together with the stalk or just the rolled up leaves. Season. Serve with ice.	**Carrage**
120 g (4 oz) spinach *½ of an apple* *½ tsp lemon juice* *lemon juice, sugar, salt* *2 ice cubes*	Press the spinach and apple. Add lemon juice, season and serve with ice.	**Spinach Cocktail**
120 g (4 oz) spinach *125 ml (5 fl.oz) pasteurized milk* *1 tsp lemon juice* *1 tsp sugar* *ice cubes*	Press the spinach. Shake together with the other ingredients and serve with ice.	**Spinach Milk**
200 g (7 oz) fresh, raw spinach *¼ of an onion* *½ a slice of raw celery* *½ bunch parsley* *salt, Worcester sauce*	Wash the spinach and press with the onion, celery and parsley. Mix well and season.	**Spinach Juice**
150 g (5 oz) spinach *150 g (5 oz) carrots* *100 ml (4 fl.oz) pasteurized milk* *1 tbsp lemon juice* *sugar, paprika*	Press the spinach and carrots. Shake together with the milk and lemon juice. Season with sugar and paprika.	**Spinot**
2 tomatoes *40 g (1½ oz) onion* *2 sprigs parsley* *freshly-milled pepper*	Peel the onion, wash the tomatoes and parsley. Blend everything together, mix well and add some pepper.	**Tomato and Onion Juice**

Beetroot and Apple Juice	*100 ml (4 fl.oz) beetroot juice* *100 ml (4 fl.oz) apple juice* *ground ginger*	Shake the beetroot and apple juices well. Season with a little ginger.
Tonutmeg Juice	*250 g (9 oz) tomatoes* *2 tbsps lemon juice* *a pinch each of sugar, salt,* *paprika and nutmeg*	Liquidize the tomatoes, mix well with the lemon juice and season.
Tomato Juice Bouillon	*250 g (9 oz) tomatoes* *50 ml (2 fl.oz) meat stock* *1 clove garlic* *a pinch each of marjoram and* *thyme* *a little chopped parsley*	Liquidize the tomatoes and garlic. Shake well with the herbs and stock.
Tomato and Basil Cocktail	*150 g (5 oz) tomatoes* *¼ of a cucumber* *4 basil leave* *a pinch of salt* *ice cubes*	Liquidize the tomatoes, cucumber and basil. Season with salt and pour over crushed ice.
Tomato and Sauerkraut Mix	*200 g (7 oz) tomatoes* *250 g (9 oz) sauerkraut* *½ of an apple* *a little chopped caraway* *ice cubes*	Liquidize the tomatoes, sauerkraut and apple. Shake well with ice. Strain and serve with a little caraway.
Carromix	*100 ml (4 fl.oz) carrot juice* *50 ml (2 fl.oz) each, celery, apple* *and orange juice* *a pinch of cayenne*	Shake the juices well with ice. Strain and sprinkle with a little cayenne.
Crepple	*150 g (5 oz) watercress* *100 g (4 oz) apples* *salt, mixed spices, sugar* *ice cubes*	Press the watercress and apples. Season well and serve with ice cubes.

Nucarro – Tomato and Spinach Juice – Tomato Juice a l'Italienne –
Cucumber and Rhubarb Juice

Celery and Apple Juice	80 ml (3 fl.oz) celery juice 120 ml (5 fl.oz) apple juice 1 tsp lemon juice ice cubes	Shake all the juices well with ice cubes. Strain and serve.
Celery Power	50 ml (2 fl.oz) celery juice 50 ml (2 fl.oz) tomato purée 20 ml (1 fl.oz) lemon juice ice cubes sea salt freshly-milled pepper	Shake the juices and purée well with ice cubes. Season with freshly-milled pepper.
Celery Milk	100 ml (4 fl.oz) celery juice 50 ml (2 fl.oz) pasteurized milk 1 tbsp cream celery salt, pepper chopped parsley	Shake everything together well and season.
Carrot and Spinach Cocktail	200 g (7 oz) carrots 150 g (5 oz) spinach leaves 1 apple 1 tbsp lemon juice	Press the carrots, apple and spinach leaves. Season with lemon juice.
Red Cucumber Cocktail	250 g (9 oz) cucumber 1 tbsp tomato purée a pinch of garlic salt dill tips	Press the cucumber, mix well with the tomato purée and garlic salt. Sprinkle with dill tips.
Lemumber	200 g (7 oz) cucumber 2 tbsps lemon juice ½ tsp finely chopped dill mixed spices, salt ice cubes	Press the cucumber. Mix with the lemon juice, dill and ice cubes. Season.
Basumber	125 g (4 oz) cucumber 125 g (4 oz) tomatoes 4 basil leaves 1 tsp lemon juice sugar, salt, Tabasco sauce ice cubes	Press the cucumber, tomatoes and basil. Add the lemon juice and seasoning. Serve with ice.

Fruit and vegetable drinks

Fruit and vegetables in liquid form

As our awareness of healthy eating has grown so, in direct proportion, are fruit and vegetable juices enjoying increasing popularity. Their vital components act as a real pick-me-up. This is why they are enjoyed at breakfast time, as a tonic between meals, as an aperitif or even as a diet meal. To add a little variation, the numerous health juices can, without much effort, be seasoned and refined with the addition of spices and fresh produce.
The quality and freshness of the produce plays a decisive role when making juices. The fruit and vegetables used should preferably be organically grown and those rich in vitamins should be the first choice.

Garden Juice

50 ml (2 fl.oz) beetroot juice
50 ml (2 fl.oz) carrot juice
40 ml (1½ fl.oz) grapefruit juice
40 ml (1½ fl.oz) grapefruit slices
a little parsley
salt
a slice of lemon

Mix the juices and slices of grapefruit with the parsley. Season with salt and garnish with the slice of lemon.

Celery Juice with Basil

1 l (40 fl.oz) celery juice
fresh basil and celery leaves
freshly milled pepper
a pinch each of salt and
    mixed spices

Mix the celery juice and leaves well, season.

Tomato and Apple Juice

150 ml (6 fl.oz) tomato juice
100 ml (4 fl.oz) apple juice
a little ground ginger
a slice of apple
1 ice cube

Mix the juices well and pour over ice. Sprinkle with ginger and garnish with the slice of apple.

Strawberry Juice

100 ml (4 fl.oz) strawberry juice
50 ml (2 fl.oz) each orange and
    lemon juice
sugar to taste
3 ice cubes
strips of melon

Mix the juices and sugar well. Put ice cubes into a glass and pour on the juice. Garnish with strips of melon.

Orange Raspbo

100 ml (4 fl.oz) raspberry juice
100 ml (4 fl.oz) orange juice
1 tbsp lemon juice
1 tsp peeled lemon cubes
honey
2 ice cubes

Crush the ice and shake together with the juices, 1 tsp of liquid honey and the lemon cubes in a beaker.

Blackberry and Lemon Juice

150 ml (6 fl.oz) blackberry juice
100 ml (4 fl.oz) apple juice
½ tbsp sugar
3 tbsps lemon juice
ice cubes

Dissolve the sugar in the lemon juice. Mix with the blackberry and apple juices. Serve with ice.

*Garden Juice – Celery Juice with Basil – Tomato and Apple Juice –
Strawberry Juice – Orange Raspbo*

Morello Cherry and Cream Cheese	150 ml (6 fl.oz) morello cherry juice 100 ml (4 fl.oz) orange juice 1 tsp cream cheese a pinch of nutmeg	Mix the juices and cream cheese thoroughly. Season.
Blackcurrant Tea	100 ml (4 fl.oz) blackcurrant juice 125 ml (5 fl.oz) rose hip tea sugar to taste ½ tsp lemon juice	Mix together the iced, sweetened tea with the blackcurrant and lemon juices.
Tomato and Sauerkraut Cocktail	150 ml (6 fl.oz) tomato juice 100 ml (4 fl.oz) sauerkraut juice a dash of Worcester sauce a dash of lemon juice	Mix the juices well. Season and serve chilled.
Beetroot and Redcurrant Juice	150 ml (6 fl.oz) beetroot juice 100 ml (4 fl.oz) redcurrant juice ground ginger salt	Mix the juices well and season with a little ginger and salt.
Carrot Juice with Mustard	150 ml (6 fl.oz) carrot juice pinch of mustard freshly-ground pepper ice cubes	Mix everything together well and serve with ice.
Carrot Juice with Lovage	150 ml (6 fl.oz) carrot juice 100 ml (4 fl.oz) celery juice 3 lovage leaves	Mix everything together well and serve without ice.
Redcurrant and Banana Juice	150 ml (6 fl.oz) redcurrant juice 100 ml (4 fl.oz) blackcurrant juice ½ a banana	Mix the banana and redcurrant juice together and beat together with the blackcurrant juice.
Elderberry and Black	150 ml (6 fl.oz) elderberry juice 100 ml (4 fl.oz) blackberry juice 1 tsp fine sugar ½ tsp lemon juice a pinch of cinnamon	Mix the sugar, cinnamon and lemon juice and stir well into the juices.

Fruit Concentrates and Dessert Sauces

Strawberry frappés in winter

Fruit cocktails spoil us with their powerful aromas and are energy-giving pick-me-ups. So we do not want to have to do without them in winter. Using liquid fruit concentrates from a tube we can, at any time of year and without stores of fresh fruit, quickly turn out delicious fruit drinks. With the help of fruit concentrates and dessert sauces we can conjure up the most exquisite strawberry, apricot and raspberry frappés with fruit pulp or even mocha and chocolate shakes in a trice. With just a gentle squeeze of the tube we can decorate puddings or desserts and give them that delicious aroma at the same time. And, of course, we can also add that little extra to various drinks to set the gourmets' mouths watering with just one glance at them.

Spiced Apricot	2 tbsps apricot concentrate a pinch each of cinnamon and ground cloves 170 ml (7 fl.oz) milk ice cubes	Shake all the ingredients and serve with ice.
Rasbit	1½ tbsps raspberry concentrate 3 chopped peppermint leaves 150 ml (6 fl.oz) bitter lemon	Stir the raspberry concentrate and peppermint leaves together. Top up with bitter lemon. Serve with a straw.
Choc Orange	2 tbsps chocolate concentrate 120 ml (5 fl.oz) natural drinking yogurt 50 ml (2 fl.oz) orange juice ice cubes	Shake the chocolate concentrate, drinking yogurt and orange juice. Serve with ice.
Mocha Nut	2 tbsps mocha concentrate 1 tbsp ground hazelnuts 1 scoop vanilla ice cream 120 ml (5 fl.oz) milk	Mix all the ingredients together.
Berry Juice	1½ tbsps strawberry concentrate 1 tbsp raspberry concentrate 1 tbsp lemon juice 70 ml (3½ fl.oz) apple juice	Stir together the strawberry and raspberry concentrates with the lemon juice. Top up with apple juice.
Almicot	2 tbsps apricot concentrate 1 tsp lemon juice 1-2 drops almond essence 170 ml (7 fl.oz) mineral water	Stir together the apricot concentrate, lemon juice and almond essence. Top up with mineral water.
Strawberry and Grape	2 tbsps strawberry concentrate a little pepper and coriander 120 ml (5 fl.oz) grape juice 50 ml (2 fl.oz) mineral water ice cubes	Shake the ingredients well. Serve with ice.
Aprivan	2 tbsps apricot concentrate 1 scoop pistachio ice cream 120 ml (5 fl.oz) natural drinking yogurt	Mix all the ingredients together.

 Spiced Apricot – Rasbit (tall glass) – Choc Orange –
Mocha Nut (tall glass) – Berry Juice

Mochapine	*2 tbsps mocha concentrate* *a slice of pineapple* *1 tbsp drinking chocolate powder* *150 ml (6 fl.oz) milk*	Mix all the ingredients together.
Mochagrape	*2 tbsps mocha concentrate* *100 ml (4 fl.oz) natural* * drinking yogurt* *100 ml (4 fl.oz) grapefruit* * mineral water*	Stir the mocha and the drinking yogurt together. Top up with mineral water.
Mochati	*2 tbsps mocha concentrate* *50 ml (2 fl.oz) peach nectar* *120 ml (5 fl.oz) cold* * drinking chocolate* *ice cubes*	Shake all the ingredients and serve with ice.
Chocoban	*2 tbsps chocolate concentrate* *½ a banana* *50 ml (2 fl.oz) milk* *75 ml (3 fl.oz) mineral water* *ice cubes*	Mix the chocolate concentrate, banana and milk. Top up with mineral water and serve with ice.
Chocafe	*3 tbsps chocolate concentrate* *150 ml (6 fl.oz) cold coffee* *4 tbsps cream* *a pinch each of cinnamon and* * ground cloves*	Shake together all the ingredients.
Chotea	*1½ tbsps chocolate concentrate* *150 ml (6 fl.oz) cold* * peppermint tea* *ice cubes*	Stir together the chocolate concentrate and peppermint tea and serve with ice.
Raspberry Milk	*2 tbsps raspberry concentrate* *a pinch of ginger* *3 tbsps low fat fromage frais* *100 ml (4 fl.oz) milk*	Shake all the ingredients well.
Peach Melba	*2 tbsps raspberry concentrate* *50 ml (2 fl.oz) peach nectar* *120 ml (5 fl.oz) natural* * drinking yogurt*	Shake all the ingredients well.

Herbs and Spices

"Your health" with herbs and spices

If you think herbs and spices are only for seasoning food then you are wrong. The most diverse drinks can be perfumed excellently with some "green stuff". Herbs and spices give a drink that particular character which makes each glass smell and taste attractive, aromatic, and even oriental. Even so, you should not let the natural tastes and scents of the herbs and spices overpower the character of the drink itself, but rather bring it out and support it. The same drink can, if made with various herbs and spices, taste completely different, as each herb has its own character. Given this, it is no longer difficult to be creative and invent individual and original cocktails. A little delicate experimentation and mixing will certainly be rewarded. In the end, an essential "ingredient" of any cocktail is, of course, its presentation. A garnish of fresh leaves and sprigs from the herb garden will give these already special drinks a more exclusive touch. However, it is not just the culinary value of herbs that is worth noting, but also their healthiness. Some stimulate the metabolism, others are good for the blood or help digestion, some will lull you to sleep, while others will invigorate you. Nor should we underestimate their often very high content of valuable vitamins and trace elements. These greens, fresh from your garden or dried, can be used to make drinks that are both healthy and attractive.

Rostom
3 small sprigs of rosemary
2 tomatoes
a clove of garlic
freshly milled pepper

Liquidize the rosemary, tomatoes and garlic. Season with pepper.

Sagele
2 sage leaves, finely chopped
100 ml (4 fl.oz) apple juice
100 ml (4 fl.oz) red grape juice
ice cubes

Stir the ingredients together well. Serve with ice.

Pemel
6 small peppermint leaves
350 g (12 oz) melon
1 tsp lemon juice
ice cubes

Liquidize the peppermint leaves and melon. Season with lemon juice and serve with ice.

Paragrap
a bunch of parsley
1½ apples
100 g (4 oz) grapes
ice cubes

Liquidize the parsley, apples and grapes. Serve with ice.

Fraises Epices
40 g (2 oz) strawberry syrup
ground cloves, nutmeg,
   cinnamon, pepper
50 ml (2 fl.oz) white grape juice
100 ml (4 fl.oz) mineral water

Stir together the strawberry syrup, spices and grape juice. Top up with mineral water.

Peppermint Juice with Strawberries
2 fresh peppermint leaves
100 ml (4 fl.oz) apple juice
30 g (1 oz) strawberries
8 g (¼ oz) sugar
1 ice cube

Mix the apple juice, peppermint, strawberries and sugar together well. Pour over ice.

Balm Mix
2-3 fresh lemon balm leaves
150 ml (6 fl.oz) apple juice
½ a slice of pineapple
20 g (1 oz) raspberries
ice cubes

Mix the juice, pineapple, raspberries and balm together well. Pour over ice.

Rostom – Sagele – Pemel – Paragrap – Fraises Epices

Apple Power
150 ml (6 fl.oz) apple juice
juice from ½ a lemon and
    ½ an orange
1 tbsp liquid honey
½ tsp cinnamon

Mix the honey, lemon and orange juices. Add the cinnamon and apple juice and stir well.

Apple and Onion Juice
250 g (9 oz) apples
½ an onion
¼ tsp ginger
some chives

Peel the onion and liquidize with the apple. Season with ginger and sprinkle with chives.

Thytomca
½ bunch of thyme
3 basil leaves
2 tomatoes
300 g (10 oz) potatoes
Worcester sauce, salt, pepper

Liquidize the thyme, basil, tomatoes and potatoes. Season.

Dicu
3 small sprigs of dill
300 g (10 oz) cucumber
garlic salt
ice cubes

Liquidize the dill and cucumber. Season and serve with ice.

Animi
1 tsp aniseed
1 egg
1 tbsp honey
120 ml (5 fl.oz) milk

Crush the aniseed and shake with the egg, milk and honey.

Vanira
½ a vanilla pod, slit open
1 tbsp each fromage frais and
    coffee cream
150 ml (6 fl.oz) low fat raspberry
    drinking yogurt
sweetener to taste

Scrape out the vanilla pod and shake the pulp with the remaining ingredients.

Ginpear
½ tsp ground ginger
100 ml (4 fl.oz) pear nectar
100 ml (4 fl.oz) apple juice

Shake all the ingredients well.

Cardaro
¼ tsp ground cardamom
150 ml (6 fl.oz) carrot juice
2 tbsps cream
1 tbsp honey

Shake all the ingredients together.

Hot Punch

Every hot punch has its own special character

Hot punches are particularly good on cool summer evenings or even in winter. Being hot they are good for warming you up; and they also taste very good. There are many ways to make a delicious punch. The widespread notion that punch must automatically be alcohol-based is out of date since the taste of a punch is primarily determined by the choice of fruits and spices. The most commonly used ingredients are cloves, cinnamon, ginger, bay leaves, vanilla pods, various fruits and fruit peels and these lend each punch its own and occasionally very distinct character. As a base for punches you can use processed products but also various fruit juices, tea or even milk, all of which are particularly suitable. There is a practically endless variety of possibilities.

When serving a punch you should make sure that it stays hot. Preferably, you should make the punch as it was made in days gone by, in a heat resistant container (a copper kettle for example) which can then be placed on a hot plate to keep hot for a good long time. If you cannot do this then you can put the ready made punch into a vacuum flask in the kitchen. That way it will still steam when pouring out a second glass and can be enjoyed to the full. The following punch recipes are for 4 people.

Cherry Punch

300 ml (10 fl.oz) cherry juice
juice of 2 lemons
½ a lemon, sliced
200 ml (8 fl.oz) water
1 tbsp sugar
200 ml (8 fl.oz) mineral water

Bring the cherry juice and lemon juice to the boil in the sugar and water. Add finely sliced lemon and the mineral water. Serve warm.

Apple Magic

600 ml (20 fl.oz) apple juice
2 tsps sugar
a pinch of salt
3 half sticks of cinnamon
5 cloves
1 lemon

Bring the apple juice and all other ingredients to the boil. Leave for 10 minutes and strain. Cut the lemon in half lengthways, slice thinly and divide among glasses. Pour in the apple juice. Serve warm.

Raspberry Punch

250 ml (9 fl.oz) black tea
1 tbsp raspberry syrup
350ml (22 fl.oz) elderberry juice
1 lemon, rind and juice
1 clove
½ a cinnamon stick
sugar

Bring everything except the syrup and sugar to the boil. Strain, add the sugar and syrup, and serve hot.

Redcurrant Punch

600 ml (20 fl.oz) redcurrant syrup
3 tsps grenadine syrup
⅓ finely chopped vanilla pod
a lemon
a pinch each of nutmeg, ground
   cloves and cinnamon
honey

Put a thin slice of lemon into each glass. Bring all the ingredients slowly to the boil and let it stand for 3 minutes. Strain into the glasses and sweeten with honey.

Grape and Honey

50 g (2 oz) Twinings Apple Tea
300 ml (10 fl.oz) water
300 ml (10 fl.oz) grape juice
juice of an orange
a pinch each of cardamom, mace,
   and cinnamon
1 clove
2 tsps honey

Slowly bring everything to the boil. Let it stand for 3-4 minutes, strain and serve hot.

Cherry Punch – Apple Magic – Raspberry Punch

Milk Tea Punch

1 tsp black tea leaves
a pinch of nutmeg
a pinch each of cinnamon and
  ground cloves
200 ml (8 fl.oz) water
400 ml (16 fl.oz) milk
2 egg yolks
sugar

Bring the tea leaves, spices and water to the boil. Let it stand briefly and strain. Heat the milk gently and beat in the egg yolks until frothy. Mix the two, sweeten and serve warm.

Peacora

600 ml (20 fl.oz) peach nectar
1 tbsp orange syrup
4 eggs
ground cinnamon

Beat the syrup, 100 ml (4 fl.oz) of peach nectar and the eggs in a double boiler until frothy. Gradually stir in the remaining lightly-heated peach nectar. Pour into glasses and sprinkle with cinnamon.

Lime Blossom Punch

2 bags lime blossom tea
200 ml (8 fl.oz) water
½ a lemon, rind and juice
juice of ½ an orange
400 ml (16 fl.oz) red grape juice
sugar

Brew the tea in the water and lemon rind and let it draw for 4 minutes. Strain. Add the fruit and grape juices. Return to boil and sweeten to taste.

Blossom Punch

3 bags fruit peel tea
500 ml (20 fl.oz) water
½ a vanilla pod
100 ml (4 fl.oz) apple juice
sugar, lemon juice

Brew the tea bags and vanilla pulp in boiling water. Let it draw for 3 minutes. Remove bags, add apple juice, season with sugar and lemon juice.

Elder Punch

300 ml (10 fl.oz) elderberry syrup
300 ml (10 fl.oz) apple juice
juice of a lemon
3 tbsps sugar

Heat everything together. Let it stand for a while and serve hot.

Mulled Apple Juice

500 ml (20 fl.oz) apple juice
2 cloves
½ cinammon stick
peel of ½ an orange
juice of an orange
4 tsps sugar

Heat the apple juice, cloves, cinnamon and orange peel and let it stand briefly. Strain. Mix the orange juice and sugar, pour into glasses and pour on the apple juice.

Coke, Fanta, Sprite

Soft drinks are part of the "American way of life"

At the turn of the century alcohol-free soft drinks gradually began to challenge the whiskies of the Western age in the United States. It did not take very long for the "softies" to shape the "American way of life" to a decisive extent. The biggest contribution to this development was probably made by a single product which, after the two world wars, established itself in Europe and other parts of the world at a whirlwind pace. At this time, people were very open to things from the New World and anybody who was anybody drank Coca-Cola. In the interim, the "dark lemonade" has made history, a history, however, on which the final page has yet to close. Quite the opposite, it continues to expand as recently Sprite and Fanta have joined it too – to make sure there really is something for all "tastes". As part of the slimming wave, low calorie drinks have been welcomed with enthusiasm and so began Coca-Cola's second conquering of the world, this time with its "Diet" label. In its wake the new Diet Sprite with its refreshing lemon taste has begun its victory march, too.
After more than a century of "Coke", as the Americans call it, it is right to ask just why this drink is so popular with both young and old. One reason for this, apart from its unmistakable taste, is certainly the refreshing, invigorating, and even slightly stimulating effect of this caffeine-containing drink.
However, we should also not forget the fact that the name Coca-Cola no longer stands just for a drink but has now become a symbol. These days we associate such values as leisure, carefree living, optimism, openness and freedom with the drink – and who would not want to share in these?

Violetta
50 g (2 oz) blackberries
1 tbsp blackcurrant syrup
50 ml (2 fl.oz) ginger ale
100 ml (4 fl.oz) Sprite

Mix the blackberries, blackcurrant syrup and ginger ale. Top up with Sprite.

Peach Drink
½ a peach
1 scoop vanilla ice cream
1 tbsp cream
100 ml (4 fl.oz) Sprite

Dice the peach and put into a glass. Add the vanilla ice cream and cream. Top up with Sprite.

South Sea Magic
1-2 ice cubes
50 ml (2 fl.oz) milk
50 g (2 oz) finely sliced pineapple
1 tsp sugar
1 scoop vanilla ice cream
50 ml (2 fl.oz) Coca-Cola

Put the ice cubes into a glass. Mix the milk, pineapple, sugar and vanilla ice cream and pour into the glass. Top up with Coca-Cola.

Blond Greek
1-2 ice cubes
1 tsp lemon juice
2 tbsps orange juice
150 ml (6 fl.oz) Coca-Cola

Put the ice cubes and juices into a glass, top up with Coca-Cola.

Kon-Tiki
1 scoop orange ice cream
50 ml (2 fl.oz) milk
*1 tbsp unsweetened
  pineapple juice*
a pinch of vanilla sugar
100 ml (4 fl.oz) Coca-Cola

Put the orange ice cream into a glass. Mix the milk, pineapple syrup and vanilla sugar well and pour on. Top up with Coca-Cola.

Movie Star
1 tbsp redcurrant juice
50 ml (2 fl.oz) tonic water
150 ml (6 fl.oz) Diet Coca-Cola
2 ice cubes

Pour the redcurrant juice, tonic water and Coca-Cola into a glass. Serve with ice.

Choco-Cola
60 g (2 oz) liquid chocolate
3 ice cubes
2 tbsps condensed milk
150 ml (6 fl.oz) Coca-Cola

Mix the chocolate with the ice cubes and condensed milk. Pour into a glass, and top up with Coca-Cola.

Violetta – Peach Drink – South Sea Magic – Blond Greek

Cherry Cola

2 tsps cherry essence
1 scoop vanilla ice cream
1 tbsp milk
100 ml (4 fl.oz) Diet Coca-Cola
1 ice cube

Mix the cherry essence with the vanilla ice cream and milk. Put into a glass and top up with Diet Coca-Cola. Serve with ice.

Cola Brasilia

1 tsp instant coffee
1 tsp sugar
200 ml (8 fl.oz) Coca-Cola
1 ice cube

Stir together the coffee and sugar. Top up with Coca-Cola. Add ice and serve.

Demoiselle

50 ml (2 fl.oz) coconut milk
2 ice cubes
150 ml (6 fl.oz) Diet Coca-Cola

Put the ice cubes into a glass and pour on the coconut milk. Top up with Diet Coca-Cola.

Fakir

4 tbsps pineapple juice
vanilla sugar
150 ml (6 fl.oz) Coca-Cola
1 ice cube

Mix the pineapple juice with the vanilla sugar. Top up with Coca-Cola and serve with ice.

Caramba

2 tbsps sugar
50ml (2 fl.oz) water
50 ml (2 fl.oz) milk
1 scoop vanilla ice cream
100 ml (4 fl.oz) Coca-Cola

Brown the sugar, add water and leave to cool. Mix with milk and ice cream. Top up with Coca-Cola.

Mignon

1-2 ice cubes
100 ml (4 fl.oz) buttermilk
3 tsps sugar
juice of ½ a lemon
100 ml (4 fl.oz) Coca-Cola
a slice of lemon

Put the ice cubes into a glass. Mix the buttermilk with the sugar and lemon juice and strain into the glass. Top up with Coca-Cola. Garnish with a slice of lemon.

Banana Fun

⅓ of a banana
5 red cherries
200 ml (8 fl.oz) Fanta

Slice the banana and alternate with cherries on a toothpick. Top up with Fanta.

1 tbsp orange syrup 1 tbsp liquid chocolate 1 ice cube 2 tbsps milk 150 ml (6 fl.oz) Coca-Cola	Mix the orange syrup, chocolate, ice cubes and milk together. Pour into a glass. Top up with Coca-Cola.	**Togo**
1 scoop vanilla ice cream 50 ml (2 fl.oz) peach juice 100 ml (4 fl.oz) Fanta 1 tbsp lemon juice	Mix the vanilla ice cream with the peach juice, Fanta and lemon juice.	**Funny Kiss**
juice of ½ an orange juice of ½ a grapefruit juice of ½ a lemon 2 tbsps pineapple juice 100 ml (4 fl.oz) Fanta 1 ice cube	Press the juices, mix and top up with Fanta. Serve with ice.	**Vitamin Bomb**
flesh of ½ an orange sugar to taste 1 scoop mandarin ice cream 100 ml (4 fl.oz) Fanta	Cut the orange into small pieces, sweeten and let it stand for 1 hour. Put into glasses. Add the mandarin ice cream and top up with Fanta.	**Underground Drink**
50 ml (2 fl.oz) pineapple juice some lemon juice 150 ml (6 fl.oz) Fanta ½ slice of pineapple 1 ice cube	Mix the pineapple and lemon juices. Top up with Fanta. Garnish with the slice of pineapple.	**Pineapple Dream**
1 ice cube juice of 1 orange 150 ml (6 fl.oz) Fanta 1 slice of orange	Put the ice cubes and orange juice into a glass and top up with Fanta. Garnish with a slice of orange.	**Dishy Edgar**
1 ice cube 50 ml (2 fl.oz) pineapple juice 150 ml (6 fl.oz) Fanta some pineapple chunks	Put the ice cubes and pineapple juice into a glass. Top up with Fanta. Carefully add some pineapple chunks.	**Alhambra Dream**

Grapefruit Highball	2 tbsps grenadine syrup 7 tbsps grapefruit juice 100 ml (4 fl.oz) ginger ale	Stir the grenadine syrup and the grapefruit juice together. Top up with ginger ale.
Red Kiss	2 tbsps cranberry jam juice of 1 lemon 100 ml (4 fl.oz) tonic water 1 ice cube	Mix the cranberry jam, lemon juice and sugar together. Top up with tonic water. Serve with ice.
Sweet and Sour	juice of 1 lemon juice of ½ a grapefruit 1 tsp sugar 100 ml (4 fl.oz) bitter lemon a twirl of lemon rind	Mix the lemon juice, grapefruit juice and the sugar together. Top up with bitter lemon. Garnish with twirl of lemon.
Rose Crystal	1 ice cube 25 g (1 oz) strawberry syrup a dash of lemon juice 150 ml (6 fl.oz) Fanta	Pour the strawberry syrup and lemon juice into a glass with the ice. Top up with Fanta.
Melanie	⅛ of a melon peppermint leaves lemon juice sugar to taste 100 ml (4 fl.oz) Fanta	Scoop out balls from the melon and leave to stand in lemon juice and sugar. Top up with Fanta and serve with a spoon.
Kinky Boots	1 scoop vanilla ice cream 50 ml (2 fl.oz) bilberry juice 100 ml (4 fl.oz) Fanta a scoop of whipped cream	Put the vanilla ice and bilberry juice into a glass. Top up with Fanta. Garnish with whipped cream.
Ginger Cup	2 small pieces of ginger 2-3 drops rum essence 200 ml (8 fl.oz) tonic water 2-3 ice cubes	Put the ginger and rum essence into a glass with the tonic water. Add ice and serve.
Smooth Gabriel	1-2 ice cubes juice of 1 lemon 150 ml (6 fl.oz) Coca-Cola a slice of lemon	Put the ice cubes and lemon juice into a glass. Top up with Coca-Cola. Garnish with a slice of lemon.

 Grapefruit Highball – Red Kiss – Sweet and Sour –
Rose Crystal – Melanie

Maple Cup	2 tsps maple syrup 2 tsps orange syrup 1 tbsp yogurt 150 ml (6 fl.oz) Diet Sprite 1 ice cube	Mix the two syrups and the yogurt in a glass. Top up with Diet Sprite and add the ice cube.
Bedouin Joke	1-2 ice cubes 1 tsp instant coffee 1 tbsp sugar syrup 150 ml (6 fl.oz) Coca-Cola	Put the ice in a glass. Dissolve the coffee in a little water and pour into the glass with the syrup. Top up with Coca-Cola.
Squire's Cup	1-2 ice cubes 100 ml (4 fl.oz) tomato juice salt, pepper 100 ml (4 fl.oz) Coca-Cola	Put the ice into a glass. Season the tomato juice and pour on. Top up with Coca-Cola.
Lance Breaker	1 scoop vanilla ice cream 50 ml (2 fl.oz) grape juice 100 ml (4 fl.oz) Coca-Cola a scoop of cream	Put the vanilla ice cream into a glass and top up with grape juice and Coca-Cola. Garnish with cream.
Orange Blossom	1-2 ice cubes 50 ml (2 fl.oz) yogurt juice of 1 orange 2 tbsps sugar 100 ml (4 fl.oz) Coca-Cola	Put the ice into a glass. Mix the yogurt, orange juice and sugar and strain into the glass. Top up with Coca-Cola. Garnish with a slice of orange.
Last Dash	1 ice cube 100 ml (4 fl.oz) bilberry juice 100 ml (4 fl.oz) Coca-Cola	Put the ice into a glass. Top up with bilberry juice and Coca-Cola.
Beau	1 ice cube 50 ml (2 fl.oz) red grape juice a dash of lemon juice 100 ml (4 fl.oz) Fanta	Put the ice and juices into a glass. Top up with Fanta.
Pineapple Cup	½ a slice of pineapple 1 scoop lemon sorbet 1 tbsp cream 150 ml (6 fl.oz) Diet Sprite	Dice the pineapple finely and put into a glass with lemon sorbet and cream. Top up with Diet Sprite and mix.

40 g (1½ oz) strawberries *1 scoop strawberry ice cream* *2 tbsps strawberry syrup* *100 ml (4 fl.oz) Sprite* *2 tbsps cream*	Cut the strawberries into small cubes, add the strawberry ice cream and syrup. Top up with Sprite and top with whipped cream.	**Strawberry Cocktail**
50 g (2 oz) chocolate *2 tbsps cherry syrup* *50 ml (2 fl.oz) milk* *a little lemon juice* *100 ml (4 fl.oz) Sprite*	Melt the chocolate and pour into a glass. Mix the syrup and milk, season with lemon juice. Top up with Sprite.	**Daydream**
50 g (2 oz) wild strawberries *sugar* *juice of ½ a lemon* *150 ml (6 fl.oz) bitter lemon* *3 ice cubes*	Sugar the strawberries and leave to stand briefly in the refrigerator. Put into a glass. Trickle lemon juice over them and top up with bitter lemon. Serve with ice.	**White Shadow**
juice of 1 lemon *1 tbsp sugar syrup* *150 ml (6 fl.oz) bitter lemon* *3 ice cubes* *a slice of lemon*	Mix the lemon juice and syrup. Top up with bitter lemon. Serve with ice. Garnish with lemon slice.	**Lemon Cooler**
1 ice cube *juice of ½ a lemon* *12.5 g (½ oz) raspberry syrup* *150ml (6 fl.oz) ginger ale*	Put the ice into a glass with the lemon juice and raspberry syrup. Top up with ginger ale.	**Ginger Ale Highball**
a few ice cubes *1 tsp sugar syrup* *150 ml (6 fl.oz) ginger ale* *nutmeg*	Put the ice into a glass with the syrup. Top up with ginger ale. Sprinkle with nutmeg.	**Ginger Ale Sangaree**
25 g (1 oz) orange syrup *2 scoops orange ice cream* *25 g (1 oz) cream* *50 ml (2 fl.oz) tonic water* *cream*	Put the orange syrup, 1 scoop of ice cream and cream into a glass and three-quarters fill with tonic water. Add second scoop of ice cream and top with whipped cream. Serve with a spoon and straw.	**Orange Ice Cream Soda**

Orange Cooler

100 ml (4 fl.oz) orange juice
2 tbsps sugar
100 ml (4 fl.oz) ginger ale
3 ice cubes

Mix the orange juice and sugar together. Top up with ginger ale. Serve with ice.

Grenadine Lemonade

5 tbsps grenadine syrup
150 ml (6 fl.oz) tonic water
2 ice cubes

Put the syrup into a glass. Top up with tonic water and serve with ice.

Cucumber Mix

¼ of a cucumber
50 ml (2 fl.oz) Sprite
100 ml (4 fl.oz) tonic water

Wash and purée the cucumber with the Sprite. Top up with tonic water.

Aranciata

50 ml (2 fl.oz) orange syrup
50 ml (2 fl.oz) Fanta
150 ml (6 fl.oz) Coca-Cola

Put the orange syrup into a glass. Top up with Fanta and Coca-Cola.

C-Cup

1 lemon, prepared
1 tsp icing (confectioner's) sugar
50 ml (2 fl.oz) Diet Coca-Cola
100 ml (4 fl.oz) Diet Sprite

Mix the slices of lemon with the sugar and leave to stand for a while. Top up with Coca-Cola and Sprite.

Reton

40 g (1½ oz) redcurrants
50 ml (2 fl.oz) tonic water
150 ml (6 fl.oz) bitter lemon

De-stalk the redcurrants and put into a glass. Pour on the tonic water and bitter lemon.

Kiwi Bitter

1 kiwi fruit
50 ml (2 fl.oz) Sprite
150 ml (6 fl.oz) bitter lemon

Peel the kiwi fruit and remove a slice. Dice the remaining fruit and put into a glass. Top up with Sprite and bitter lemon. Garnish glass with the slice of kiwi fruit. Serve with a spoon.

Creme d'Apricot

2 tbsps apricot nectar
2 tbsps cream
50 ml (2 fl.oz) Coca-Cola
100 ml (4 fl.oz) Fanta

Mix the apricot nectar with the cream and Coca-Cola. Top up with Fanta.

Ginger Dream

a small piece of fresh ginger root
100 ml (4 fl.oz) ginger ale
100 ml (4 fl.oz) tonic water

Wash the ginger root and chop finely. Pour on the ginger ale and let it stand for a while. Strain and top up with tonic water.

1 lime *1 tsp icing (confectioner's) sugar* *150 ml (6 fl.oz) Diet Sprite*	Cut the lime in half and remove 1 slice. Press and mix with sugar. Top up with Diet Sprite and decorate glass with lime.	**Limelight**
juice of ½ an orange *1 tbsp raspberry purée* *150 ml (6 fl.oz) Diet Coca-Cola* *1 ice cube*	Mix the orange juice and purée together in a glass. Top up with Diet Coca-Cola. Add ice.	**Idyll**
1 tbsp lemon juice *3 tbsps pineapple juice* *200 ml (8 fl.oz) Diet Coca-Cola* *ice cubes*	Mix the juices in a glass and top up with Diet Coca-Cola. Serve with ice.	**Colapino**
20 g (1 oz) raspberries *1 ice cube* *juice of ½ a grapefruit* *150 ml (6 fl.oz) Diet Sprite*	Mix the raspberries and ice. Put in a glass with the grapefruit juice and Diet Sprite.	**Raspberry Dry**
3 tbsps pineapple purée *2 tbsps lemon juice* *Diet Coca-Cola* *2 ice cubes*	Mix the pineapple purée and lemon juice in a glass. Top up with Diet Coca-Cola and serve with ice.	**Cocapeach**
25 g (1 oz) pineapple syrup *ice* *50 ml (2 fl.oz) tonic water* *1 scoop pineapple ice cream* *½ a slice of pineapple*	Put the pineapple syrup into a glass and two-thirds fill with ice. Pour on tonic water. Add the ice cream and garnish with pineapple. Serve with a straw and spoon.	**Pineapple Freeze**
1 ice cube *juice of 1 lemon* *2 tsps sugar syrup* *150 ml (6 fl.oz) ginger ale* *slice of lemon* *fruit*	Put the ice into a glass with lemon juice and syrup. Top up with ginger ale. Garnish with slice of lemon and fruit.	**Brunswick Cooler**

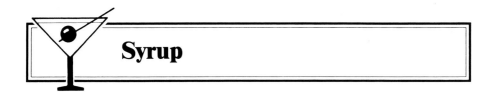

Syrup

Syrup – a seductive magician

The once highly popular syrups made from fruit, blossoms, and other parts of plants have now fallen somewhat into neglect. And yet, syrups can make the most delicious drinks which stand out not just because of their taste and aroma but also for their bright appearance. Eyes sparkle and palates tingle for this intensely appealing delight. Syrup is truly an all-round drink. Properly prepared, a syrup will be well received by everyone. Children like it straight; but adults often have to be reintroduced to that real syrup taste before learning to enjoy it again. And this will be no problem at all. The multitude of varieties allow you to mix the most exclusive cocktails that are in no way second to their alcoholic counterparts.

Served with ice in summer and boiling water in winter, syrup is an all year round winner. It can be diluted with the most diverse drinks. Syrup is also excellent for sweetening tea, for combining with fruit juices, or for adding that extra taste to dairy products. With syrup it is easy to bring both variety and change into your drinks cabinet.

 *Rosele Hip – Strawberry Mint – Raspberry Yellow – Minger –
Gren-Girup*

Rosele Syrup

40 g (1½ oz) rose hip syrup
½ an apple
1 tbsp lemon juice
mineral water

Peel and grate the apple and mix with the syrup and lemon juice. Top up with mineral water.

Strawberry Mint

40 g (1½ oz) strawberry syrup
a little grated candied sugar
4 fresh peppermint leaves
1 tbsp lemon juice
150 ml (6 fl. oz) mineral water

Mix the peppermint leaves with the syrup, sugar and lemon juice. Top up with mineral water and serve with ice.

Raspberry Yellow

40 g (1½ oz) raspberry syrup
1 egg yolk
2 tbsps cream
mineral water
ice cubes

Shake everything well. Top up with mineral water and serve with ice.

Minger

40 g (1½ oz) peppermint syrup
a pinch of ginger
1 tbsp lemon juice
150 ml (6 fl. oz) mineral water

Mix everything well and serve chilled.

Gren-Girup

40 g (1½ oz) grenadine syrup
100 ml (4 fl. oz) grapefruit juice
crushed ice
mineral water

Mix everything well. Top up with mineral water.

Raspberry Tea

40 g (1½ oz) raspberry syrup
100 ml (4 fl. oz) cold black tea
2 leaves of peppermint
mineral water

Let the peppermint cool in the tea. Mix with the syrup. Top up with mineral water and serve with ice.

Pemello

40 g (1½ oz) peppermint syrup
1 scoop melon ice cream
1 tbsp lemon juice
mineral water

Shake the syrup, melon ice cream and lemon juice and top up with mineral water.

20 g (¾ oz) grapefruit syrup *20 g (¾ oz) raspberry syrup* *1 tbsp lemon juice* *a little grated lemon rind* *50 ml (2 fl.oz) apple juice* *mineral water*	Mix everything well and top up with mineral water.	**Graspberry**
40 g (1½ oz) lemon syrup *½ of a stewed apricot* *1 small scoop lemon sorbet* *mineral water*	Mix the syrup with the peach and sorbet. Top up with mineral water.	**Lemopeach**
20 g (¾ oz) pineapple syrup *20 g (¾ oz) strawberry syrup* *orangeade* *ice cubes*	Mix the syrups well. Add ice cubes and top up with orangeade.	**Sunshine**
20 g (¾ oz) blackcurrant syrup *2 drops almond essence* *100 ml (4 fl.oz) white grape juice* *mineral water* *ice cubes*	Mix everything well and top up with mineral water.	**Grabla**
40 g (1½ oz) blood orange syrup *1 tbsp lemon juice* *100 ml (4 fl.oz) apple juice* *50 ml (2 fl.oz) mineral water*	Mix everything well and serve chilled.	**Paradiso**
40 g (1½ oz) strawberry syrup *1 tbsp each lemon and* * orange juice* *150ml (6 fl.oz) mineral water* *ice cubes*	Shake everything well and serve with ice.	**Southberry**

Chermon	40 g (1½ oz) cherry syrup 2 tsps lemon juice 125 ml (5 fl. oz) apple juice ice cubes	Mix everything well and serve with ice.
Redap	40 g (1½ oz) redcurrant syrup 1 tsp lemon juice 100 ml (4 fl. oz) apple juice ice cubes	Shake everything well and serve chilled.
Aprico	40 g (1½ oz) apricot syrup 1 tsp honey 1½ tbsps lemon juice mineral water ice cubes	Mix everything well and top up with mineral water.
Elder Cream	40 g (1½ oz) elderberry syrup 1 small scoop vanilla ice cream 1 tbsp cream lemon mineral water	Shake everything well and top up with lemon mineral water.
Redcurrant and Orange	40 g (1½ oz) redcurrant syrup 100 ml (4 fl. oz) orange juice ice cubes mineral water	Mix everything well and top up with mineral water.
Blackira	40 g (1½ oz) blackcurrant syrup 1 tbsp each orange juice and lemon juice 150o ml (6 fl. oz) mineral water ice cubes	Shake everything well and serve with ice.
Blacky	20 g (¾ oz) cherry syrup 20 g (¾ oz) redcurrant syrup 1 tbsp lemon juice mineral water ice cubes	Mix everything well. Top up with mineral water and serve with ice.

 Graspberry – Lemopeach – Sunshine – Grabla – Paradiso

Rogra Juice	40 g (1½ oz) rose hip syrup 4 tbsps grapefruit juice crushed ice mineral water	Shake everything well and top up with mineral water.
Limerose	40 g (1½ oz) rose hip syrup 1 tbsp lime juice a little grated lime peel 100 ml (4 fl.oz) white grape juice mineral water	Shake the syrup, lime juice and peel and the grape juice. Top up with mineral water.
Almondberry	40 g (1½ oz) strawberry syrup 2-3 drops almond essence crushed ice 150 ml (6 fl.oz) mineral water	Mix everything well and top up with mineral water.
Grenale	40 g (1½ oz) grenadine syrup crushed ice 150 ml (6 fl.oz) ginger ale	Mix everything well and serve chilled.
Grevanill	40 g (1½ oz) grenadine syrup 1 scoop vanilla ice cream 1 tsp ground hazelnuts mineral water	Shake everything well and top up with mineral water.
Grapele	40 g (1½ oz) grapefruit syrup 40 g (1½ oz) grape juice lemon mineral water ice cubes	Mix the syrup and juice well. Top up with mineral water and serve with ice.
Granilla	40 g (1½ oz) grapefruit syrup ½ tsp orange syrup a little ground cloves and cinnamon mineral water	Mix everything well and top up with mineral water.

40 g (1½ oz) raspberry syrup *2-3 drops vanilla essence* *1 scoop pistachio ice cream* *mineral water*	Shake the syrup, vanilla essence and pistachio ice cream well. Top up with mineral water.	**Raspanilla**
40 g (1½ oz) lemon syrup *1 tsp liquid honey* *a pinch of cinnamon* *150 ml (6 fl.oz) mineral water* *crushed ice*	Shake everything well and serve with ice.	**Lemberry**
40 g (1½ oz) lemon syrup *⅓ of a banana* *a pinch of ground cloves* *mineral water*	Mix the syrup and banana well. Season and top up with mineral water.	**Banamon**
40 g (1½ oz) orange syrup *a pinch of mace* *crushed ice* *150 ml (6 fl.oz) mineral water*	Mix the syrup well with the mace and ice. Top up with mineral water.	**Nucora**
40 g (1½ oz) orange syrup *a pinch each of cinnamon and ground cloves* *1 tbsp lemon juice* *mineral water*	Shake everything well and top up with mineral water.	**Clolemo**
25 g (1 oz) each pineapple and orange syrup *4 tbsps lemon juice* *mineral water* *ice cubes*	Mix everything well. Top up with mineral water and serve with ice.	**Andora**
40 g (1½ oz) blackcurrant syrup *1 tbsp lemon juice* *1 scoop lemon sorbet* *100 ml (4 fl.oz) apple juice* *4 blackberries*	Mix the syrup and lemon juice. Add sorbet. Top up with apple juice and garnish with the blackberries.	**Black and Blue**

Chernilla	*40 g (1½ oz) cherry syrup* *50 ml (2 fl.oz) milk* *1 tbsp vanilla ice cream* *mineral water*	Shake everything well. Top up with mineral water and serve chilled.
Chercoa	*40 g (1½ oz) cherry syrup* *1 tsp chocolate powder* *1 tsp ground hazelnuts* *1 egg yolk* *80 ml (3 fl.oz) milk* *1 tbsp crushed ice*	Shake everything well.
Redclove	*40 g (1½ oz) redcurrant syrup* *50 ml (2 fl.oz) apple juice* *a pinch of ground cloves* *mineral water* *ice cubes*	Mix everything together well. Serve with ice and top up with mineral water.
Elderegg	*20 g (¾ oz) elderberry syrup* *2 tbsps each orange and lemon juice* *1 tsp honey* *1 egg* *mineral water*	Mix everything well. Shake. Serve with ice and top up with mineral water.
Rosele	*40 g (1½ oz) elderberry syrup* *150 ml (6 fl.oz) apple juice* *ice cubes*	Mix everything well and serve chilled.
Rosale	*40 g (1½ oz) elderberry syrup* *1 tbsp lemon juice* *ginger ale* *crushed ice*	Mix everything well and serve chilled.
Lemora	*40 g (1½ oz) lemon syrup* *100 ml (4 fl.oz) orange juice* *mineral water*	Mix everything well and top up with mineral water.

Chermon – Redap – Aprico – Elder Cream –
Redcurrant and Orange

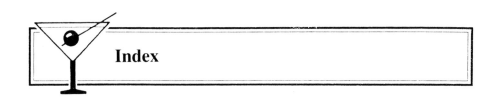

Index

 Limelight – Idyll – Colapino – Raspberry Dry – Cocapeach